SCHOLASTIC

PRIMARY SOURCES
FOR THE INTERACTIVE WHITEBOARD

Colonial America   Westward Movement   Civil War

Karen Baicker

New York • Toronto • London • Auckland • Sydney
Mexico City • New Delhi • Hong Kong • Buenos Aires

Teaching Resources

Edited by Sarah Longhi
Cover design by Jay Namerow
Interior and interactive whiteboard activity design by Maria Lilja

ISBN: 978-0-545-25793-0

2 3 4 5 6 7 8 9 10   40   18 17 16 15 14 13 12 11

CONTENTS

CIVL WAR

REPRODUCIBLES

Introduction

PRIMARY SOURCES: MAKING SENSE OF HISTORY

Primary sources are the unforgettable voices and indelible images from the past that add texture and perspective to our understanding of history.

Through letters, journals, photographs, advertisements, and other artifacts, students are able to experience a slice of history directly and form their own impressions of a historical event or figure. This experience can dramatically enhance the second-hand descriptions and interpretations that textbooks provide, which students often find difficult and tedious to read.

Interacting With Primary Sources

Just as primary sources bring history to life, the interactive whiteboard brings primary sources to life!

Looking at an image of the actual Mayflower Compact, penned in the script of its time and yellowed with age, one is struck that the words were inscribed by real people, with a vision for their own government. But, to many students, the document may still be a flat, static image on the page. Through these interactive whiteboard lessons, however, students can hear the Compact read aloud, explore the meaning of different passages, get a glossary pop-up, and access Web links to learn more. The primary source springs to life, and with it, history.

The interactive whiteboard presents primary sources in a highly engaging, multidimensional way. It's possible to enlarge documents, zoom in on or otherwise highlight specific sections, listen to certain words and passages, and link to supporting Web sites—all while retaining the integrity of the original sources. This book and CD of primary sources enable you to guide your students through colonial diaries, Civil War letters, pioneer journals, historic speeches, and much more. Additionally, interactive maps and time lines allow you to give context, placing each document in time and space.

With a large, interactive display and countless opportunities for collaborative learning, using an interactive whiteboard is an effective, engaging way to teach students the skills they'll need to succeed in the 21st century: interpreting visual aids, marking text, synthesizing information, organizing data, evaluating Web sites, and team work. These skills are also an increasingly important part of the Common Core State Standards. Using this dynamic tool is a perfect way to motivate even your most reluctant learner.

The resources have been designed to harness what the interactive whiteboard does best!

Research has shown that the interactive whiteboard is most effective when it is used to engage students in active, hands-on learning with meaningful activities. Each featured activity encourages students to reflect on the document, interact with the material and with each other, and draw their own connections—all hallmarks of effective instruction.

ABOUT THIS RESOURCE

WHAT'S INSIDE

- **Inside the book,** you'll find teaching suggestions and background information for all the documents presented in the interactive whiteboard files. You'll also find reproducible activity pages to use with the documents.

- **The companion CD** features the primary source documents on individual pages, intended for use with a Promethean ActivBoard. It also includes interactive maps and time lines, interactive files for each primary source, and PDFs of each document to print or project. Additionally, the CD offers featured activities designed to engage students in interactive exploration, such as picture tours with audio narration.

The primary sources provided offer your students the chance to experience history firsthand—in all of its genuine, real-life detail. Students will encounter the words of ordinary children and adults living in the 18th and 19th centuries. They will read from the letters and diaries of some of our country's most influential early leaders. Finally, they will understand the difficulties and great opportunities presented by living through the early years of our nation.

Your students will benefit most from working with these documents when you help to set a context and engage them with critical viewing and thinking activities. Students can prepare for an exploration of any of the documents in this collection by completing the Evaluate That Document! form (page 96). This form helps students evaluate a primary source by guiding them to identify important document characteristics and pose questions prior to the class activity. Reproduce it from the book, print it from the CD, or open it on your interactive whiteboard.

The Teaching Notes section for each document provides tips for exploring the resource on the interactive whiteboard, teaching suggestions, and background information. (You'll also find these notes easily accessible in the Notes column of the Flipchart.) Some documents, such as the Mayflower Compact (page 22), feature text that is difficult to read. For these, as well as for lengthy documents or in cases where images of original documents were not available, we have included typeset transcriptions along with the original. You'll find them on tabs in the Flipchart.

The CD contains an ActivInspire Flipchart file for each section of the book: Colonial America, Westward Movement, and Civil War. Each Flipchart contains a page with a primary source document and teaching notes that help you guide students to analyze the document with the whiteboard's general tools, such as the Pen and Magnifier. In addition, there are eight to ten Featured Activities for each unit that provide an even more dynamic use of the whiteboard, including matching games, drag-and-drop sorting activities, and fill-in-the-blanks. Students can complete maps, write captions, analyze photographs, listen to speeches, view picture tours, and much more. Extra tabs include bonus content to enrich the resource.

Teaching Primary Sources With the ActivInspire Files

Download the ready-to-go Flipchart files onto the computer that connects to the interactive whiteboard. Use the menu to select the activity you'd like to use.

Whether you and your students are already adept at using an interactive whiteboard or have just decided to give it a try, you will find these fun, dynamic activities straightforward and easy to use.

Although some of the documents offer structured activity, the best way to use the interactive whiteboard is to keep your lessons open and flexible to your own classroom needs. Here are some general tips for working with these files:

- Target a specific era or historical focus and select one or more of the related primary source documents in this resource.

- Locate events related to the documents on the interactive time line, encouraging students to add their own dates and events in blank bubbles.

- Use the interactive map to present a geographical context for the documents. Mark important locations with the Pen tool or highlight them on the map.

- Display the documents and have students jot notes or talk with a partner about their initial reaction and what they think they know about the document.

- Read the Teaching Notes provided for the documents and share historical background with students.

- Revisit the documents and encourage students to interact with them using whiteboard tools or the featured interactive activities.

- Have students evaluate and review the documents. You may want to have students fill out the Evaluate That Document! activity sheet (page 96) or simply use it as a prompt to guide their analysis.

- Help students connect the documents and their new understandings to the broader study of the period. You might use this as a jumping-off point for introducing connected events, reviewing other documents related to the area of study, evaluating documents that present a different point of view, or helping students gather related sources for a larger project or unit study.

NOTE: If you don't already have ActivInspire software, you can access a free personal version after registering with Promethean Planet (www.prometheanplanet.com). For more information, click the links you'll find on the PDF included on the CD.

Tech Tips

If you are still getting the hang of your ActivBoard, be sure to look at the tips online at Promethean Planet. To help students navigate the documents, we have created specific toolbar palettes for each activity. The following is an overview of the main ActivInspire features you may also use with these activities. All are available in the toolbox unless otherwise noted.

SPECIAL FEATURES FOR THIS RESOURCE

For easy access, you'll find these interactive tools at the bottom of most activity page screens:

Magnifier Select this tool, then click and hold to enlarge a document. Double click the screen to return to the full-size view.

Scroll Arrow This symbol prompts you to click on the featured document and drag it upward to view the entire image or text.

Reset (See description at right.)

Print Doc Clicking this button allows you to print the on-screen document.

Main Menu Clicking this button returns you to the menu screen.

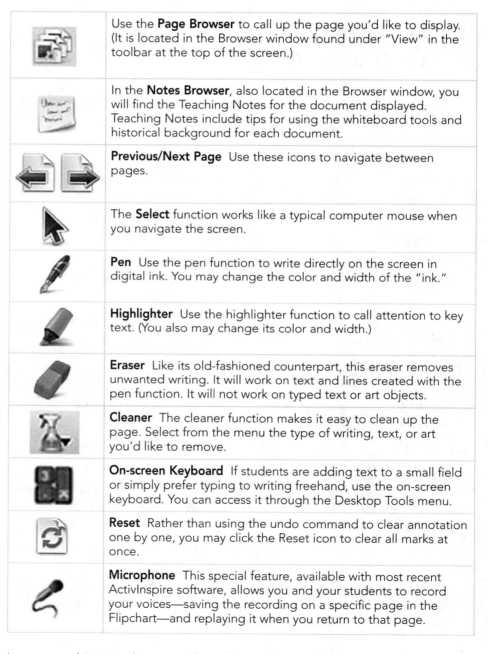

	Use the **Page Browser** to call up the page you'd like to display. (It is located in the Browser window found under "View" in the toolbar at the top of the screen.)
	In the **Notes Browser**, also located in the Browser window, you will find the Teaching Notes for the document displayed. Teaching Notes include tips for using the whiteboard tools and historical background for each document.
	Previous/Next Page Use these icons to navigate between pages.
	The **Select** function works like a typical computer mouse when you navigate the screen.
	Pen Use the pen function to write directly on the screen in digital ink. You may change the color and width of the "ink."
	Highlighter Use the highlighter function to call attention to key text. (You also may change its color and width.)
	Eraser Like its old-fashioned counterpart, this eraser removes unwanted writing. It will work on text and lines created with the pen function. It will not work on typed text or art objects.
	Cleaner The cleaner function makes it easy to clean up the page. Select from the menu the type of writing, text, or art you'd like to remove.
	On-screen Keyboard If students are adding text to a small field or simply prefer typing to writing freehand, use the on-screen keyboard. You can access it through the Desktop Tools menu.
	Reset Rather than using the undo command to clear annotation one by one, you may click the Reset icon to clear all marks at once.
	Microphone This special feature, available with most recent ActivInspire software, allows you and your students to record your voices—saving the recording on a specific page in the Flipchart—and replaying it when you return to that page.

Icons are subject to change as the software is upgraded.

Colonial America

OVERVIEW

Until about 400 years ago, little changed in North America from one year to the next. The land was inhabited by dozens of Native American tribes, whose traditions carried on through gradual adaptations. The arrival of European settlers around 1600 changed those ways of life abruptly and permanently. Our continent has been changing dramatically ever since. In fact, the changes have been so radical that your students may have trouble understanding what life was like in the Colonial era. Primary sources can help.

Many of today's social issues first surfaced during colonial times. Then as now, people with vastly different backgrounds lived together. Europeans, Native Americans, and Africans forged a shared, often strained, sometimes violent coexistence. The successes and failures of that profound intermingling continue to define our culture.

The first Africans entered the colonies in 1619 as indentured servants. Their arrival led to the birth of slavery in the colonies and that, too, is a legacy we still struggle with today.

Religion played a central role in the development of the United States, providing cultural cohesiveness in the early colonial period. From those first seekers of religious freedom, Americans have inherited a respect for religion and its power. But they also have a fundamental belief in the importance of separating church and state functions. This belief is born, in part, of the witch hunts and trials of the late 1600s.

And, of course, pre–Revolutionary America provides us with a wealth of information on the relationship between a colony and the mother country. The economic needs of Britain and the colonies, as well as the political struggles of each, become apparent as we read the documents of the time.

Colonial America Time Line (c. 1607–1775)

1607
Friendly relations develop between British Captain John Smith, leader of the Jamestown colony, and Powhatan, leader of several Algonquin Indian tribes

1609–1610
The Jamestown colony faces "the starving time;" of the 214 colonists, only 60 survive

1619
The first colonial legislature, Virginia's House of Burgesses, is established; the first Africans arrive as indentured servants

1620
Pilgrims sign the Mayflower Compact and found Plymouth colony in Massachusetts; Massasoit, leader of the Wampanoag tribe, meets the Pilgrims

1621
Massasoit signs a peace treaty with the Pilgrims

1636
The first colonial college, Harvard, is founded in Massachusetts

1660
Indentured Africans become slaves for life in Jamestown

1675–1676
Metacomet (King Philip) leads Native Americans in war against the New England colonists

1681
William Penn founds Pennsylvania

1690
The first New England primer is printed

1692
Salem witch trials and executions are conducted

1730–1740s
The Great Awakening, a series of religious revivals, takes place

1754
The Albany Plan of Union is proposed by Benjamin Franklin but rejected by the colonies

1754–1763
The French and Indian War is fought mainly between France and England with the support of Native American allies on both sides; Britain wins, gaining control of land from the Atlantic Ocean to the Mississippi River

1765
Britain's Parliament passes the Stamp Act and the Quartering Act

1766
Benjamin Franklin testifies to Parliament against the Stamp Act and Parliament repeals it

1767
Parliament passes the Townsend Acts, which tax tea and other goods

1768
British troops arrive in Boston to maintain law and order

1770
Five colonists, including one African-American man, are killed by British troops in the Boston Massacre

1773
During the Boston Tea Party, colonists protest tax on tea by dumping 342 chests of British Tea into Boston Harbor

1773
Poetry of Phillis Wheatley, a slave, is first published

1773
Parliament passes the Quebec Act, granting religious freedom only to Roman Catholics

1774
The First Continental Congress meets in Philadelphia

1775
The battles of Lexington and Concord are fought; the Second Continental Congress meets and names George Washington commander in chief of the American troops fighting against Great Britain

TEACHING NOTES

Colonial America Time Line

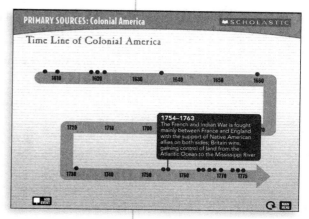

FEATURED INTERACTIVE ACTIVITY

Use this interactive time line to preview milestones of the Colonial era. Return to it to provide context for documents as you explore the primary sources in this collection.

Click the dots to read about key events of Colonial America. To add your own event, drag a bubble shape from the **Add Event** button to the time line and use the **Pen** or **On-screen Keyboard** tool to write in a description.

Map of the American Colonies

FEATURED INTERACTIVE ACTIVITY

Use this map activity to explore the location of key places during Colonial America. Return to the map as you explore the primary sources to provide geographic context for each document.

Map 1: Map of the American Colonies, 1750

1. Drag the labels of each colony to the corresponding boxes on the map.

2. Click **Reveal Answers** to check the answers or to see the map filled in without completing the activity.

3. Click the **Next** arrow to explore Map 2.

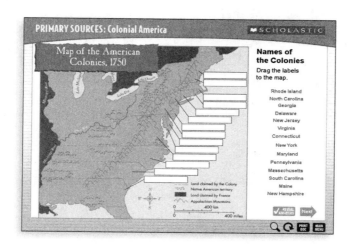

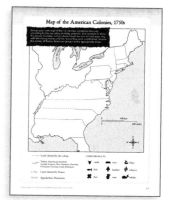

See page 91 for a reproducible map activity sheet. Answer Key, page 92.

Map 2: Map of the American Colonies, 1750: Native American Territories

1. The Native American territories listed at right are hidden on the map. Have students use the **Eraser** tool to reveal their locations.

2. Click the **Reset** button to let other students try the same activity and time themselves.

3. Click the **Next** arrow to explore Map 3.

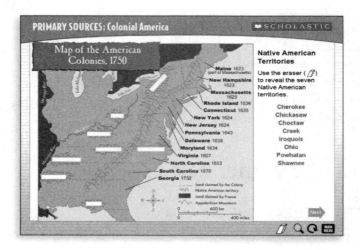

Map 3: Map of the American Colonies, 1750: Chief Products

1. Have students drag the icons of different resources to the name that matches below.

2. Students can then click each word to see the resource appear on the map.

A Briefe and True Report: 1588

BACKGROUND INFORMATION

Thomas Hariot was born in 1560 in Oxford, England. A true Renaissance man, Hariot was a mathematician, scientist, scholar, and writer. He helped Galileo invent the telescope.

Hariot lived in the home of Sir Walter Raleigh as a tutor of math and science to sea captains. When Raleigh set out to establish the first permanent English colony in America, he brought Hariot along to record the history of the journey.

This report is a summary of their journey and the settlement of Roanoke Island in what is now North Carolina. The Roanoke colony was the first English-speaking settlement in the New World. It failed under mysterious circumstances around 1590. Jamestown became the first successful English colony.

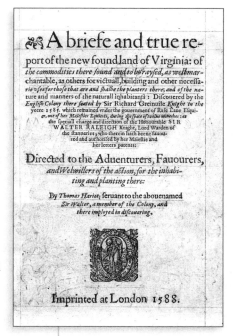

INTERACTIVE ACTIVITY

Use the interactive tools to explore this firsthand report of the journey to America and settlement of Roanoke Island.

1. Look at the *Briefe and True Report* cover together.

2. Point out the portrait of Thomas Hariot and share some background information on the writer of this document.

3. Click the **Excerpt** button to read a transcript of part of the report.

4. Click the **Web Link** button to find the complete text and original art.

Activity screens

TIPS

- Use the **Magnifier** tool to zoom in on the cover and explore the different handwriting and spelling in the report cover, such as the elongated letter *s* in *necessarie*.

- Use the **Pen** tool to let students rewrite sentences in their own words and with modern spellings.

- Record students reading parts of the report using the **Microphone** tool, if available.

The Village of Secota: 1590

BACKGROUND INFORMATION

John White was a cartographer and draftsman at Roanoke, and he drew a diagram of a Native American village (the Powhatan village called Secota on the drawing) for Thomas Hariot's "Report." German engraver Theodore de Bry then made this engraving based on John White's drawing.

The engraving reveals the sophistication and order of the village. The corn is shown in three different stages of growth, revealing staggered harvesting times. There are other crops as well, including squash, pumpkins, and tobacco. The activity in the center depicts trade among other Native Americans and with Europeans. The drawing also shows places for prayer, ceremony, and burial as well as dwellings.

Letters were included on the original engraving, likely added by Hariot and described in the test. A legend on the engraving was supplied in 1960 by historian Richard L. Morton.

FEATURED INTERACTIVE ACTIVITY

Use this activity to explore an early engraving of a Native American village.

Purpose: Examine a diagram closely to gain information about a late 16th century Native American culture described from a European perspective.

1. Look at the *Village of Secota* document together. Discuss what the different areas of the diagram depict.

2. Click the **Activity** button to interact with the diagram. Have students fill in the legend on the right using the letter labels from the engraving.

3. For clues, click near each letter on the engraving and read the hints that pop up.

4. After students have filled in the legend with their guesses, click the **Reveal Answers** button to discover the correct answers.

5. Click the tabs along the left side to read more about the daily life, culture and religion, and agriculture of the Powhatan.

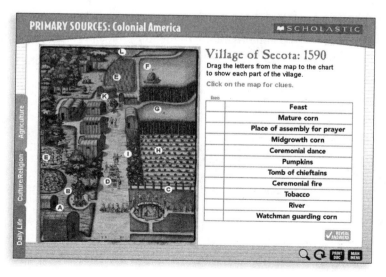

The Starving Time: 1609–1610

BACKGROUND INFORMATION

Founded in 1607 with the hopes of finding and exporting gold, Jamestown was the first permanent British colony in the New World. Captain John Smith was its

first leader. The first seven months proved quite difficult. Of the original 214 colonists, only 60 survived disease and famine. The Powhatan offered the colonists much-needed assistance, giving them corn and bread. However, the relationship became more complex as time went on. The Powhatan became angry when the colonists did not return their generosity. Some colonists stole from them, further damaging relations.

Smith played a critical role in establishing good relations with Wahunsonacock, the Powhatan leader, and in requiring that all colonists work. However, many in the original group of colonists had come from Britain's gentry class and were unaccustomed to work; they were hoping to find easy gold.

The winter of 1609–1610 became known as "The Starving Time." Historians are uncertain exactly what caused this horrible situation. We do know that Captain Smith had returned to England, leaving the colony under the leadership of George Percy and John Rolfe, and relations with the Powhatan were tense (see Wahunsonacock's 1609 speech, next page). In addition, the winter was harsh. Armed Powhatans laid siege to Jamestown, preventing settlers from leaving the stockaded area. (The 19th-century painting overlaying the transcription excerpt suggests how the fort may have looked.) Buildings were burned to create warmth. Many people starved to death.

Activity screens

INTERACTIVE ACTIVITY

Use the interactive tools to explore the journal entry of a Jamestown colonist.

1. Look at the painting together and discuss how the fort may have looked.

2. Click the **Transcript** tab to read a survivor's account. (Be aware that the content contains descriptions of cannibalism, for which you may want to prepare students in advance of the reading.)

3. Invite students to identify words that are spelled differently than we spell them today.

4. Have students compare and contrast what they've learned about Roanoke and Jamestown.

TIPS

- Use the **Magnifier** tool to zoom in on different features in the painting of the fort.

- Insert a new page and have students use the **Pen** tool to rewrite sentences in their own words.

- Record students reading parts of the journal entry using the **Microphone** tool, if available.

"Why Should You Take by Force What You Can Have by Love?": 1609

BACKGROUND INFORMATION

The English colonists relied on the help of the Powhatan Confederacy. When the relationship was not reciprocated, the Powhatan leader, Wahunsonacock, made this plea for respect and cooperation. His words were copied down by Captain John Smith before he left for England—just before The Starving Time.

Note that the coloring on this image was added after the original engraving was made.

INTERACTIVE ACTIVITY

Use the interactive tools to explore a Powhatan leader's speech, recorded by Captain John Smith.

1. Look at the *Why Should You Take by Force…?* speech together. Also examine the engraving of a Powhatan leader, created two years before Wahunsonacock's speech.

2. Invite students to notice each time Wahunsonacock asks a *why* question. What does each of these questions reveal about the Powhatan people's beliefs and values?

3. Ask students to read the speech aloud. Have them pause and restate the points that Wahunsonacock was trying to make.

4. Compare this document with the journal entry of a Jamestown colonist.

Activity screens

TIPS

- Record students reading parts of the report using the **Microphone** tool, if available.

- Insert a new page and have students use the **Pen** tool to rewrite sentences in their own words.

- Use the **Magnifier** tool to read the caption of the engraving. Have students examine how Powhatan is depicted and discuss what the image shows about Powhatan's relationship to his people.

The First Thanksgiving Proclamation: 1676

BACKGROUND INFORMATION

The history of Thanksgiving is rife with myth and competing claims. Accounts exist describing a feast in 1621 in Plymouth. On December 12, 1621, Edward Winslow wrote a letter describing the event in a positive light (see excerpt). This feast was not repeated the following year or made official until a proclamation was issued in 1676, in Charlestown, Massachusetts (main document).

INTERACTIVE ACTIVITY

Use the interactive tools to explore this official proclamation of one of the earliest Thanksgivings.

1. Look at the primary source image of the actual proclamation together.

2. Click the **Transcript** tab to read the text more easily.

3. As students read the proclamation, pause to explore what the language reveals about the values and beliefs of the colonists.

4. Have students identify the things the colonists were grateful for and fearful of. Discuss the fact that much of the proclamation focuses on gratitude for having successfully overcome their enemies—the "Heathen Natives," a sentiment that runs contrary to common perceptions about Thanksgiving. Invite them to share what they had predicted the colonists might be grateful for.

5. Click the **Account from 1621** tab to read an account of a harvest feast from 55 years earlier. Encourage students to contrast the two documents. Ask how the focus of the colonists' language has changed and why they think this might be.

TIPS

- Zoom in on the proclamation using the **Magnifier** tool.

- Use the **Pen** tool to let students rewrite sentences in their own words and with modern spellings.

- Record students reading parts of the proclamation using the **Microphone** tool, if available.

- Use the **Highlighter** tool with different colors to show what the colonists were grateful for and fearful of.

Activity screens

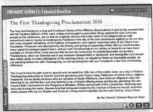

Diary of Mary Osgood Sumner as a Child: Late 1700s

BACKGROUND INFORMATION

It was common for colonial children to keep journals or monitors. These pages from a child's monitor show how religious ideals ran through every fiber of daily life. Mary Osgood Sumner divided her monitor so that the left page was, as she called it, her black leaf, and the right page, her white leaf. On the left page she recorded every mistake or sin she committed during the day, while on the white page she listed the good and dutiful things she had done.

FEATURED INTERACTIVE ACTIVITY

Use this activity to explore the diary of a colonial child.

Purpose: Examine the primary source to make inferences about the culture and values of the colonists around 1700.

1. Explore the diary entry and discuss the format of the black leaf/white leaf monitor, in which "good" actions are listed on the right and "bad" thoughts or deeds listed on the left. Ask students what they find most striking.

2. Click the **Activity** button to allow students to interact with the diary page.

3. Ask students to read along as they listen to the diary excerpts. (Click the **Audio** button.) Hover over the highlighted terms to reveal what they mean.

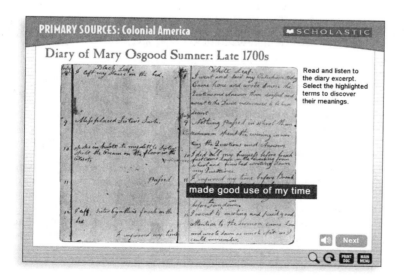

4. Go to the next page for a fill-in-the blank activity. Ask students to drag words from the word bank to fill in the blanks. Phrases will stay in place when they are correct.

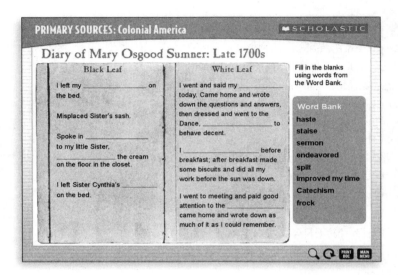

The Great Awakening: 1730s and 1740s

BACKGROUND INFORMATION

The Great Awakening was an outburst of Christian religious zeal in the early 1700s. It was highlighted by a series of revivals led by men like George Whitefield (pronounced WHIT-field), a Methodist preacher from England. Whitefield (1714–1770) was considered the greatest evangelist of his time. Evangelicals like Whitefield believed that people could be converted from a state of sin to a "new birth" through the preaching of scripture.

During the Great Awakening, Whitefield made seven tours of Colonial America. As many as 30,000 people might have attended just one of his outdoor sermons. He even used a collapsible, portable pulpit, like the one shown here, to make his job easier. Other ministers, such as Jonathan Edwards of Massachusetts and Theodore J. Frelinghuysen of New Jersey also stirred believers with their preaching.

The Great Awakening began in Connecticut and spread to the southern colonies throughout the second half of the 1700s and into the 1800s. The surge in religious fervor caused splits within several Christian denominations, including the Congregationalists and the Quakers.

The excerpt shown with Whitefield's portrait was taken from a sermon entitled "Marks of a True Conversion." The oil portrait was painted by Joseph Badger some time between 1743 and 1765.

INTERACTIVE ACTIVITY

Use the interactive tools to explore the Great Awakening through primary sources.

1. Look at the oil portrait of George Whitefield as you give students some background about the Great Awakening.

2. Click the **Excerpt** tab to share a selection from the sermon, "Marks of a True Conversion."

3. Look at the collapsible, portable pulpit and discuss what it reveals about the evangelical movement of the early 1700s.

TIPS

• Zoom in on the portrait of Whitefield and the collapsible pulpit using the **Magnifier** tool.

• Use the **Highlighter** tool to identify phrases from the sermon excerpt that are intended to be persuasive.

• Connect to the Library of Congress "Religion and the Founding of the American Republic" online exhibition at **www.loc.gov/exhibits/religion/ religion.html** to build more background about Whitefield, his evangelical contemporaries, and The Great Awakening under "Religion in Eighteenth-Century America."

Activity screens

The Mayflower Compact: 1620

BACKGROUND INFORMATION

The Mayflower Compact was the first effective agreement for democratic self-government in North America. When the Pilgrims landed at Plymouth in 1620, they realized that they would need to select leaders and draft laws in order to live in a peaceful, orderly society. Each man aboard the Mayflower signed the document, pledging to abide by decisions made as a group, even if he did not agree with all aspects of these decisions. The Mayflower Compact has been called the first American constitution.

The document was first published in 1622 in *Mourt's Relation: A Journal of the Pilgrims at Plymouth*. The original version has been lost. William Bradford wrote a copy of the Mayflower Compact in his *History of Plimoth Plantation* in 1630. That is the copy shown here.

FEATURED INTERACTIVE ACTIVITY

Use this activity to explore the document considered by many to be the first American constitution.

Purpose: Build comprehension through rephrasing original text.

1. Look at the Mayflower Compact document together. To hear the document read aloud, click the **Audio** button.

2. Click the **Transcript** tab to read the document in modern type. Hover over any word in red to reveal a glossary definition. Ask students to take turns reading the document and discussing its meaning. Note that the **Painting** tab provides a secondary source description of the signing by N. C. Wyeth (1939).

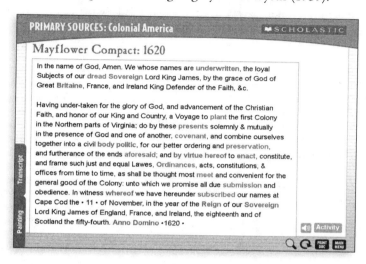

3. Click the **Activity** button to engage students in a multiple-choice activity. For the first question, read the brief excerpt from the Mayflower Compact. Ask students to infer the best meaning of the excerpt. You can take a show of hands, or have students write their answers down. Then click the **Reveal Answer** button to discover the correct answer. Move on to the next question by clicking the **Next** button, or selecting one of the numbered tabs on the left.

4. Allow students to make up their own restatements as well. You can use the **Pen** tool to write their statements on the board.

5. Once they have carefully read the document, make sure students can identify the main goal of establishing the first British colony in this part of the world and the authors' religious and political justifications for doing so.

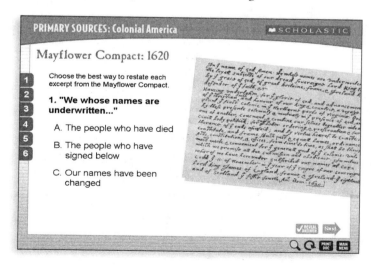

Capital Laws: 1672

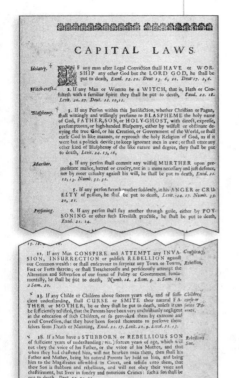

BACKGROUND INFORMATION

Capital punishment laws carry a possible death sentence for violators. This partial list of "Capital Laws" is taken from *The General Laws and Liberties of the Massachusetts Colony*, published in 1672. The laws demonstrate the importance of religion in the lives of the early colonists. This document, printed in Cambridge, Massachusetts, cites the Bible passages upon which each of these laws is based. In contrast to the capital laws, many civil laws that the colonists adopted were based on English common law.

INTERACTIVE ACTIVITY

Use the interactive tools to examine some of the laws that governed the lives of early colonists in Massachusetts.

1. Look at the Capital Laws images together. (Please preview these sections to check that they are appropriate for your class.)

2. Use the background information above to provide context and to explain that these Capital Laws carried possible death sentences.

3. Read the featured laws aloud and discuss how the colonists' laws relate to our current laws. Discuss the separation of church and state established in the United States Constitution.

Activity screen

TIPS

• Zoom in on the documents using the **Magnifier** tool.

• Use the **Spotlight** tool to explore the different handwriting and spelling in the laws.

• Have students use the **Pen** tool to rewrite sentences in their own words and with modern spellings.

• Record students reading parts of the documents using the **Microphone** tool, if available.

Town Meeting: 1721

BACKGROUND INFORMATION

Town meetings were a form of local governance strongly associated with New England. As these records from Providence, Rhode Island, show, the laws passed at town meetings were often very mundane. But the meetings gave free men an opportunity to express their views about issues of the day.

FEATURED INTERACTIVE ACTIVITY

Use this activity to explore the records of an early New England town meeting.

Purpose: Examine the document to probe the nature of town meetings and local government in the early 1700s.

1. Look at the image of a New England town meeting while reading the accompanying caption.

2. Click the **Meeting Notes** button to read the excerpt of the Providence, Rhode Island, town meeting.

3. Click the **Activity** button to have students complete a Problem and Solution T-chart based on the community issues discussed at the meeting.

4. Use the **Meeting Notes** button to refer back to the primary source document, if needed.

5. As an extension activity, invite students to conduct a mock town meeting for issues affecting your school or town. Insert a new page and have them use the **Pen** tool to complete their own Problem and Solution T-chart for the mock town meeting.

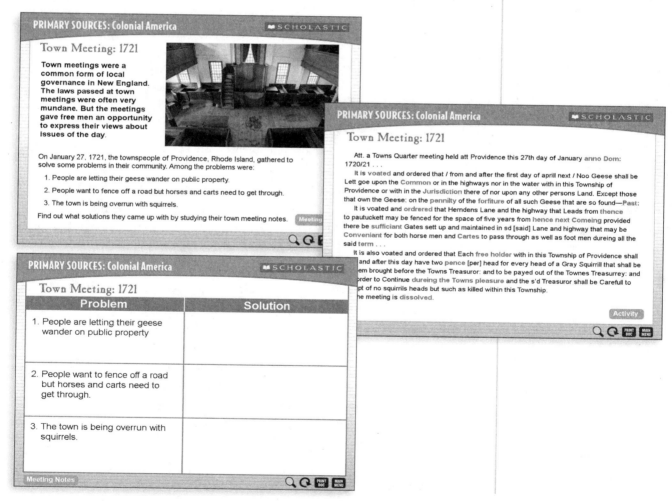

Activity screens

Trial of Mary Easty: 1692 *and* Witches' Petition for Bail: 1692

BACKGROUND INFORMATION

The close ties that existed between the political and religious life of the colony were typical in the New England colonies where Puritanism was strongest—this eventually became known as the "New England Way." Only the "visible saints" (those believed to have received God's grace) were able to vote and hold public office.

While such uniformity of belief was originally cohesive and good for the life of the colony, eventually some within the faith began to question some tenets of Puritanism. The dissension was seen by many as the work of the devil (with witches as his assistants). It left the Puritans feeling that they must get rid of the devil in their midst and examine what they might have done to bring the wrath of God upon their community.

In a sense, their deep religiosity and joining of church and state functions led to the witch-hunt hysteria. Depositions like the one shown here took place all over the colonies—Salem, Massachusetts, being only one, but the most well-known, site of witch trials. The drawing from 1880 depicts the trial of Giles Corey's wife.

These trials followed none of our contemporary basic rights of representation—and so, circumstantial evidence, hysteria, and cruelty prevailed.

INTERACTIVE ACTIVITY

Use the interactive tools to explore documents related to the witch trials that took place in the colonies in the late 1600s.

1. Look at the drawing, made in 1880, that shows a witch trial from 1692. Discuss the context of Puritanism in the colonies and the witch-hunt hysteria. Ask students what they think may have been the perspective of the illustrator about the trials.

2. Click the **Transcript** tab and have students read the deposition given at the trial of Mary Easty. Encourage students to discuss any issues they might find in this testimony being used to determine punishment. Review some of the differences between these 17th-century trials and trials today. (See the background information above.)

3. Look at the image of the Witches' Petition for Bail. Click the **Transcript** tab and have students read the petition aloud. Ask students to identify what the petitioners are requesting and their reasons for making the request.

TIPS

- Use the **Highlighter** tool to mark phrases and words in the deposition that lead students to question the veracity of the statements.

- Use the **Magnifier** tool to zoom in on the image of the witches' petition.

- Record students reading the deposition and petition with the **Microphone** tool, if available.

Diary of Anna Green Winslow: 1771

BACKGROUND INFORMATION

Most children who kept diaries wrote of religious matters and copied the tone and content of their older relatives. The diary shown here is an exception. In her journal, Anna Green Winslow wrote of her actual daily life and sometimes trivial concerns. Therefore, it has become a more valuable resource in examining the daily lives of colonial children. In this excerpt, Anna is 12 years old and living with her aunt.

INTERACTIVE ACTIVITY

Use the interactive tools to read the journal entry of a 12-year-old girl in the colonies.

1. Look closely at the photo and the diary entry of Anna Green Winslow.

2. Read the entry aloud, helping students with difficult spelling and writing. Help students see Anna's attempt at humor about wearing the red "Dominie." Can they fathom what that might look like?

3. Discuss the concerns of Anna compared to the concerns of teenagers today. How are they alike and how are they different?

4. Click the **Audio** button to hear the entry read aloud.

TIPS

- Use the **Magnifier** tool to explore some of the differences in handwriting (such as the elongated *S* and superscript letters) and spelling (*fation* for fashion; *Hatt* for hat) that may make the diary entry difficult for students to read.

- Click the **Transcript** tab to read a typeset version of the diary entry.

Activity screens

New England Primer *and* Hornbook: 1700s

BACKGROUND INFORMATION

The *New England Primer* (pronounced PRIM-er) was the most commonly used textbook in the United States for over a century. First printed in 1690, it was used as a reading book for children in the first grade. Some versions were still in use as late as 1900. The Primer included many religious references.

The primer was small in size, usually just $2\frac{1}{2}$ by 4 inches. This was due, in part, to the cost of paper and printing.

More emphasis was placed on the formal education of boys than girls, although girls received some formal education and a thorough training in all domestic affairs. It was the boys who would go on in a trade or profession, which often required literacy and math skills. Before students could use a primer, they first had to master a hornbook. The hornbook consisted of a sheet of paper inscribed with the alphabet and numbers, which was attached to a sturdy wooden paddle and covered by a protective, transparent sheet of horn. Children first learned their ABCs from the hornbook and then moved on to a primer.

FEATURED INTERACTIVE ACTIVITY

Use this activity to explore several tools used for teaching children reading as well as religious and moral values in the Colonial era.

Purpose: Examine the primer in close detail to explore education in the colonies.

1. Look at the copy of the *New England Primer*.

2. Click the **Activity** button. Have students read the primer, or click the **Audio** button to hear it read aloud.

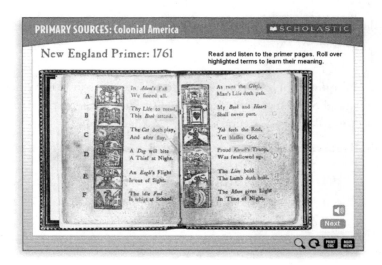

3. Hover over any word or phrase highlighted in blue to reveal its meaning.

4. Go to the next page, and have students complete the primer by moving the image or words to the appropriate spot on the page. Correct answers will stick in place, while incorrect answers will bounce back.

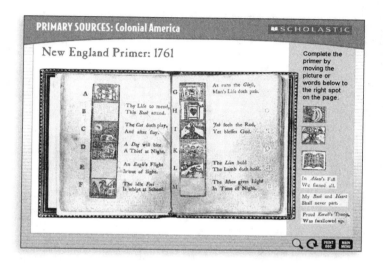

5. Click the **Hornbook** tab to see a photograph of an 18th-century paddle used to practice handwriting. Enlarge the paddle with the **Magnifier** tool and let students trace the letters with the **Pen** tool. You can also print the document (use the **Print Doc** button) and make copies for students to practice tracing the letters at their desks.

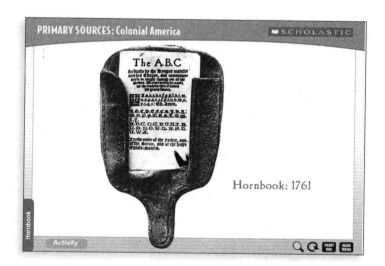

Ben Franklin's Almanac: 1733, 1750

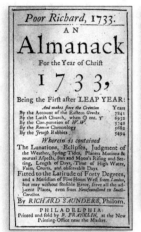

Activity screen

BACKGROUND INFORMATION

Benjamin Franklin's *Poor Richard's Almanack*, published under his pseudonym, Richard Saunders, was a bestselling book that rolled household hints, weather forecasts, scientific information, cooking recipes, and wit into one easy-to-read package. First published in 1732, the *Almanack* became a household item, eventually selling almost 10,000 copies per year.

INTERACTIVE ACTIVITY

Use the interactive tools to explore two pages from different editions of *Poor Richard's Almanack*.

1. Look at the two pages from Ben Franklin's *Poor Richard's Almanack*.

2. Discuss the role that almanacs played in the 1700s, and share some almanacs from recent years, if available.

3. Encourage students to point to details that reveal aspects of colonial life on these pages.

4. Have students identify the different signs of the zodiac around the body in the illustration. Starting at the top and moving clockwise, they are: Aries, Taurus, Cancer, Virgo, Scorpio, Capricorn, Pisces, Aquarius, Sagittarius, Libra, Leo, and Gemini.

TIPS

• Zoom in on parts of the almanac page using the **Magnifier** tool.

• Go online with students and use a search engine to locate a current Farmer's Almanac, as well as to look at other pages from *Poor Richard's Almanack*. Examine the documents together and compare and contrast the kind of information provided in early almanacs with information in almanacs published today.

Hieroglyphic Bible: 1789

BACKGROUND INFORMATION

This page is from a book called *A Curious Hieroglyphick Bible*, featuring almost five hundred woodcuts made by American artists. The publisher and printer was Isiah Thomas, who produced children's literature. Bibles such as this were used to teach the Scriptures and reading at the same time.

INTERACTIVE ACTIVITY

Use the interactive tools to explore and discuss the pages from this hieroglyphic bible.

1. Look at the words and pictures shown on these bible pages.

2. Try to read the sentences, substituting words for the pictures.

3. Encourage students to discuss how the book was used to teach reading skills and religious studies at the same time. Compare this document to the *New England Primer*, which also combined literacy instruction and religion.

4. Have students create their own rebus sentences drawing pictures to stand for different words.

TIPS

- Use the **Spotlight** tool to focus on different images on the page.

- Have students use the **Pen** tool to label the images with words.

- Insert a new page and invite students to use the **Pen** tool to create their own rebus statements and drawings.

Activity screen

Smallpox Epidemic: 1726

BACKGROUND INFORMATION

Cotton Mather was a famous minister from Boston. In 1721, a smallpox epidemic broke out in the New England colonies. Mather had heard that some doctors in Turkey had developed inoculation techniques. He urged Boston doctors to use the same techniques.

Mather recommended that people be exposed to small amounts of smallpox by rubbing the pus of smallpox victims into tiny cuts. He convinced one doctor, Zabdiel Boylston, to experiment with this treatment. Mather suffered many attacks for his controversial position, including having a bomb thrown at his home.

The experiment worked, however. Immunizations today are based on the same principle, that exposure can build immunity. The pamphlet shown (written by Boylston) was printed in London in 1726.

INTERACTIVE ACTIVITY

Use the interactive tools to explore the pamphlet regarding smallpox inoculation techniques.

1. Look at the image of the pamphlet together.

2. Share the background information about Cotton Mather. Then click the **Excerpt** tab to have students read the quotation from Cotton Mather's journal aloud.

3. Encourage students to discuss what the pamphlet reveals about medical practice and life during the early 1700s.

Activity screen

TIPS

- Have students use the **Highlighter** tool to point out specific phrases that reveal aspects of life in the colonies and the effects of smallpox.

- Use the **Microphone** tool, if available, to record Cotton Mather's journal entry.

A Narrative of the Uncommon Sufferings and Surprizing Deliverance of Briton Hammon: 1760

BACKGROUND INFORMATION

The book shown is the first independently printed slave narrative in the colonies. Briton Hammon recounts his experiences when away from his master. His adventures include being taken captive by Native Americans, by pirates, and by the British.

About six thousand slave narratives exist from the 18th century, providing a unique perspective on the lives of enslaved people in Colonial America. Some of them were published by abolitionist editors while others were published by slave owners or traders. In the 20th century, narratives of Americans who had been held as slaves in the 1800s were compiled by testimonial during the Works Progress Administration's Federal Writers' Project in the 1930s.

Activity screens

INTERACTIVE ACTIVITY

Use the interactive tools to read a firsthand account of the life of a slave.

1. Look at the excerpt from *A Narrative of the Uncommon Sufferings and Surprizing Deliverance of Briton Hammon* together.

2. Provide background on Hammon's life as well as on the genre of captivity tales.

3. Click the **Excerpt** tab to read a selection from the book.

4. Have students look for clues about whether the narrative might have been exaggerated or slanted in its point of view.

TIPS

- Use the **Microphone** tool, if available, to have students record the excerpt.

- Use the **Highlighter** tool to zero in on specific phrases for discussion, such as "good old master."

Runaway Slaves and Slave Auction: 1744, 1763

BACKGROUND INFORMATION

One indication of the miserable situations to which slaves were subjected was the posting of slave runaway notices in local papers. Some slaves were able to make it to the North, where they might pass as freemen. Often, however, they were captured and returned to their masters, who usually ordered severe punishment before returning them to their work. In the South, Native Americans came to be used as bounty hunters, although there are also many instances of Native Americans being captured and sold into slavery within the colonies and in the West Indies. This 1744 ad comes from a Charleston, South Carolina, newspaper.

The slave auction notice, also shown on this page, was printed around 1763. Notices such as these are a stark reminder of how enslaved Africans were treated as property.

Activity screen

INTERACTIVE ACTIVITY

Use the interactive tools to examine a runaway slave notice and a slave auction notice.

1. Look at the runaway slave notice from 1744, which comes from a Charleston, South Carolina, newspaper.

2. Look at the slave auction notice from 1763.

3. Look back the Smallpox pamphlet to draw conclusions about why smallpox is referred to in the slave auction notice.

4. Discuss what these documents reveal about the treatment of slaves.

TIPS

- Use the **Spotlight** tool to focus on the images used in the notices.

- Use the **Highlighter** tool to focus on different phrases. Ask students to highlight the threat implied in the runaway slave notice.

The Stamp Act: 1765

BACKGROUND INFORMATION

Between 1765 and 1770 the British Parliament passed a number of acts that steadily increased the colonists' mistrust of the British and their anger over the levies imposed by these acts. Often the acts were intended to redirect colonial purchases to the benefit of English merchants. But the colonists' protests and boycotts were so effective that Parliament repealed many of the acts.

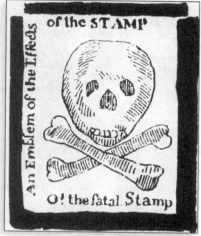

The Stamp Act was the first direct tax and affected all paper in the colonies. For every document, letter, newspaper, and license, paper embossed with the correct stamp had to be purchased from the stamp tax office. Lawyers and newspapers were especially hard hit by this tax because of the quantity of paper they used. The Act provoked such hostility that it had a unifying effect on the colonists. The poor and the wealthy were equally opposed to this tax. "Sons of Liberty" protest groups sprang up in almost every town.

The political cartoon (right) was printed on newspapers to mark the place where the stamp was to be affixed. It shows the depth of colonial hatred for the Stamp Act. A British stamp (left) is featured for contrast.

Activity screen

INTERACTIVE ACTIVITY

Use the interactive tools to explore a British stamp and a political cartoon from the period of the Stamp Act.

1. Look at the image of the British stamp and share background information about the Stamp Act.

2. Look at the political cartoon that was printed on newspapers.

3. Discuss what the cartoon reveals about the colonists' feelings about the Stamp Act.

TIPS

• Use the **Spotlight** tool to focus on the skull and to discuss what it symbolizes.

• Insert a new page and let students use the **Pen** tool to create their own political cartoon protesting the Stamp Act.

Join, or Die: 1754

BACKGROUND INFORMATION

Benjamin Franklin first inked this political cartoon as a message to the colonies during the French and Indian War. It later became the symbol of unity among the colonies and was reprinted frequently.

Each portion of the snake represents a colony. The cartoon later spawned the motto "Don't Tread on Me."

FEATURED INTERACTIVE ACTIVITY

Use this activity to explore the message behind Ben Franklin's political cartoon.

Purpose: Interpret the message expressed in the political cartoon and examine its significance to the colonists.

1. Look at the political cartoon together.

2. Click the **Activity** button. Drag the labels of the colonies from the drawing to the correct box on the map of the colonies.

3. Continue until all labels are in place, or click the **Reveal Answers** button to see the correct labels for the colonies.

4. Discuss the symbolism and why the image and motto resonated from the French and Indian war through the American Revolution and beyond.

Paul Revere's Obelisk: 1766

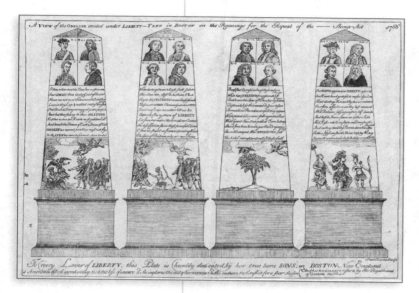

BACKGROUND INFORMATION

The Stamp Act was repealed in 1766. Paul Revere helped design an obelisk to celebrate the successful repeal of the Stamp Act. Obelisks were made with oiled paper stretched over wooden frames. They were illuminated from within by candles. Hours after Revere's obelisk was erected, it was accidentally destroyed by fire. Fortunately, Revere had made an engraving of the obelisk before the fire. The engraving, shown here, is a record of the obelisk custom and art form, as well as an account from the Revolution.

Activity screen

INTERACTIVE ACTIVITY

Use the interactive tools to examine an obelisk designed by Paul Revere to celebrate the repeal of the Stamp Act.

1. Look closely at the panels of the obelisk. Provide students with information that the obelisk itself was accidentally burned, but that this engraving remained.

2. Read the different panels and look at the illustrations.

3. Make a list of the words spelled in capitals and discuss their significance.

4. Invite students to design a panel for an obelisk to commemorate an event.

TIPS

• Use the **Magnifier** tool to examine the panels of the obelisk.

• Use the **Pen** tool to make a list of the capitalized words.

• Insert a new page and let students use the **Pen** tool to design, illustrate, and write the words for an obelisk panel.

News of an American Victory at Trenton: 1776 *and* Washington Crossing the Delaware: 1851

BACKGROUND INFORMATION

These two documents—the broadside and the painting—are paired here to help students explore the difference between a primary and a secondary source. A broadside was an announcement posted in public places. It was made from one large piece of paper and printed on one "broad side." As the broadside describes, Washington's decision to cross the Delaware took the British by surprise—in part because he and his troops made the crossing during the night and at Christmas.

The well-known painting of the event, painted by Emanuel Leutze in 1851, includes several discrepancies. For instance, it shows Washington dramatically standing up in the boat. In fact, he crossed sitting down. Also, the painting depicts the night crossing as a daytime event. And the painting shows the stars–and–stripes flag in Washington's boat. That flag was not adopted by the colonies until 1777, many months after Washington's crossing.

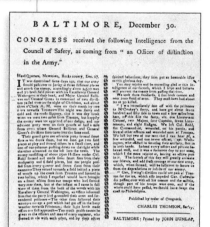

FEATURED INTERACTIVE ACTIVITY

Use this activity to explore the famous painting of George Washington crossing the Delaware River.

Purpose: Examine a painting to highlight the errors that can be introduced in a secondary source.

1. Look at Emanuel Leutze's painting of *Washington Crossing the Delaware* on Christmas day, 1776. Point out that it was painted in 1851 and contains several errors. Ask students to discuss what those errors might be.

2. Click the **Hint** buttons at the bottom of the page. Discuss what each error might be. Then click the corresponding number on the painting to learn more about it.

3. When you've reviewed the discrepancies, click the **More** button to move to the next slide. Here, discuss the concept of artistic license and why the artist may have made the choices he did in portraying the historic event.

4. Click each of the question marks to reveal more information about what each choice may have symbolized for the artist.

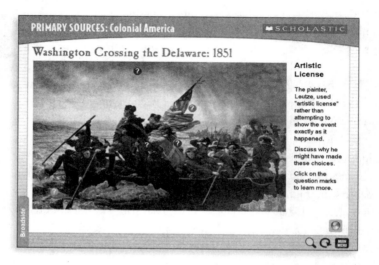

5. Click the **Broadside** tab to see a primary source account of news of the victory in Trenton in 1776. Use the pairing of these two documents to discuss the difference between primary and secondary source accounts.

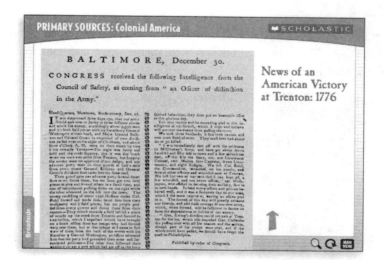

Westward Movement

OVERVIEW

The history of the United States has often been presented as one of westward movement. From the time of the explorers sailing west from Europe and reaching our shores, through the colonies, to the Mississippi, and beyond to Oregon and California, the past has been written by our westward-shifting frontiers.

More recently, increased cultural awareness has altered this perspective. The Native Americans who had lived on the land for thousands of years were not moving westward—at least not voluntarily. Nor was their world "expanding," another word frequently used to describe the westward movement. In fact, the land they knew and their resources were contracting.

Nonetheless, the events and images from this time period remain a powerful and important part of our history, and of our common culture. Elicit adjectives used to describe the pioneers—industrious, determined, brave, resourceful—and you will note characteristics still central to our national identity.

The Westward Movement is populated with colorful, legendary figures, including Daniel Boone, Davy Crockett, Wild Bill Cody, Annie Oakley, and fearless explorers such as Meriwether Lewis and William Clark. But the primary sources of ordinary people, their diaries and letters and photographs, tell an equally compelling story.

The collection of documents in The Indian Territory (pages 58–60) conveys the scope of the decimation of the Native Americans' way of life, from the slaying of buffalo for sport to holding Native American groups captive.

Westward Movement Time Line (1775–1896)

1775
Daniel Boone opens the Wilderness Road to Kentucky

1803
The Louisiana Purchase: U.S. buys Louisiana Territory from France for $15 million

1804–1806
The Lewis and Clark Expedition maps territory from Missouri to California

1807
The Clermont, Robert Fulton's steamboat, makes its first run from New York City to Albany, New York

1812
The United States declares war on Britain

The Erie Canal opens in New York

1830
The Indian Removal Act is passed

1830–1842
The Cherokee Indians are forced to move to Oklahoma via "The Trail of Tears"

1843
The first group of wagoneers travels the Oregon Trail

1845
The term "manifest destiny" is first used to justify westward expansion

1847
Mormons follow Brigham Young to Utah

1848
Gold nuggets are discovered at Sutter's Mill in California; beginning of Gold Rush

1860
The Pony Express carries mail from Missouri to California in ten days

1861
The Transcontinental telegraph line is completed

1862
The Homestead Act is created

1869
The Transcontinental Railroad is completed

1873
Barbed wire is introduced

1876
Custer is killed at the Battle of Little Bighorn in Montana

1887
Railroads create time zones to coordinate train schedules

1896
Gold is discovered in Klondike, Alaska

TEACHING NOTES

Westward Movement Time Line

FEATURED INTERACTIVE ACTIVITY

Use this interactive time line to preview milestones of the Westward Movement era. Return to it to provide context for the primary source documents in this collection.

Click the dots to read about key events of the Westward Movement. To add your own event, drag a bubble shape from the **Add Event** button to the time line and use the **Pen** or **On-screen Keyboard** tool to write in a description.

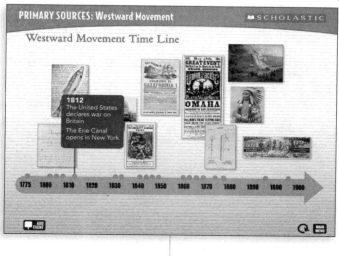

Map of the Westward Movement: 1800s

FEATURED INTERACTIVE ACTIVITY

Use this map activity to explore the location of key places during the Westward Movement. Return to the map as you explore the primary sources to provide geographic context for each document.

1. Click the buttons to see trails, the Pony Express route, and railroad lines appear on the map.

2. Explore the map's legend to determine what types of routes each line represents.

3. Discuss the geographic features that may have influenced the routes taken.

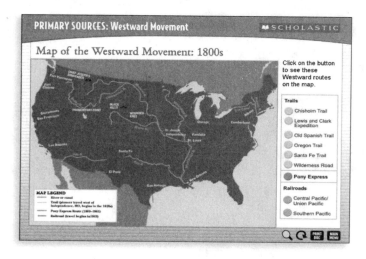

See page 95 for a reproducible map activity sheet.

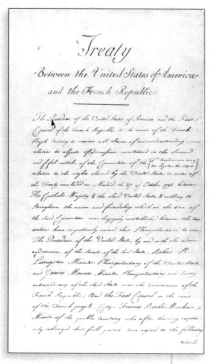

The Louisiana Purchase Treaty: 1803

BACKGROUND INFORMATION

In 1803, Louisiana was controlled by France, under the leadership of the new French emperor, Napoleon. Napoleon needed cash to fight wars in Europe, so he struck what became known as one of the greatest real estate deals in history with the United States President, Thomas Jefferson.

The signing of the Louisiana Purchase added 828,000 square miles of territory to the United States, almost doubling the size of the country for $15 million, or about 3 cents an acre. It also brought the nation back from the brink of war with Spain and France.

FEATURED INTERACTIVE ACTIVITY

Use this activity to explore how the treaty affected the United States.

Purpose: Provide geographic context for the scope of the Louisiana Purchase.

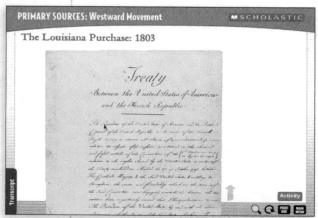

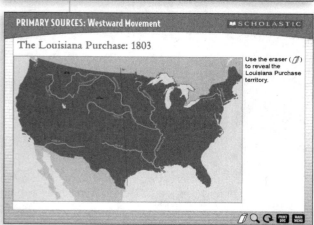

1. Look at the Treaty that certified the Louisiana Purchase. To read a selection, click the **Transcript** tab. Discuss the fact that though a treaty is only a written document, it can alter the course of history. Review the background information to help students understand the importance of this treaty.

2. Click the **Activity** button to access the map activity.

3. Have students use the **Eraser** tool to reveal the area encompassed by the Louisiana Purchase.

4. Encourage students to examine the map closely. Ask them what they notice about the borders of the territory.

The Lewis and Clark Expedition: 1804–1806

BACKGROUND INFORMATION

Following the Louisiana Purchase, President Thomas Jefferson authorized a major expedition to explore the Louisiana territory. Meriwether Lewis and William Clark led that expedition, and Jefferson charged them with making maps, keeping records of what they saw, and describing the Indians they met along the way.

The documents shown here include a photograph of their leather-bound journals; an excerpt from *The Journals of the Expedition Under the Command of Captains Lewis and Clark*; a buffalo robe the explorers sent back to Jefferson and a list of other artifacts; and some sketches from their journals. The buffalo robe is from a Mandan man, who had painted it with illustrations of a battle of the Mandans and Hidatsas against the Lakotas and the Arikaras. Jefferson displayed the robe at Monticello and it now hangs at Harvard's Peabody Museum.

FEATURED INTERACTIVE ACTIVITY

Use the activity to explore the discoveries Lewis and Clark made on their expedition.

Purpose: Gain a deeper understanding of the meaning of Lewis and Clark's expedition and the importance of the discoveries made on their journey.

1. Review the four images on the first screen.

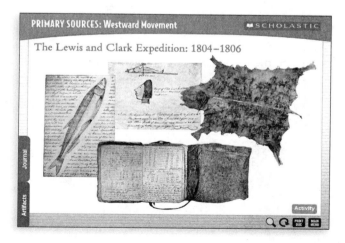

2. Click the **Journal** tab to see an excerpt from Lewis and Clark's leather-bound journals. Click the **Excerpt** button to read a journal entry transcript. Then click the **Next** button to see illustrations.

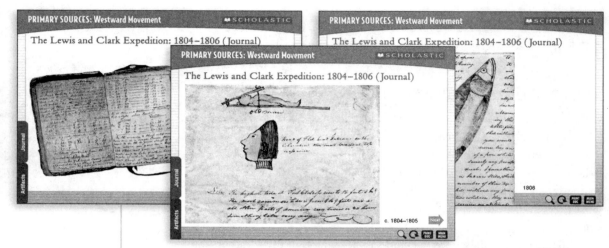

3. Click the **Artifacts** tab to see an invoice showing the contents of a package sent to Jefferson. Then click the **Next** button to see a photograph of the buffalo robe included in that shipment. Have students consider why Lewis and Clark chose to send those items and what Jefferson might have learned from them.

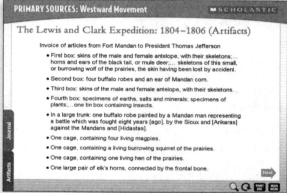

4. Click the **Activity** button to explore an interactive map of Lewis and Clark's expedition. Click the red and blue buttons to see the progression of Lewis and Clark's journey. Click the orange buttons on the map to see images of primary sources that correspond to that date and location.

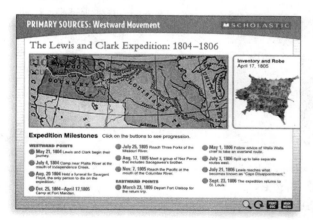

The Crockett Almanac: 1837, 1841

BACKGROUND INFORMATION

The larger document is from the cover of *The Crockett Almanac* of 1841. The small reproduction is a woodcut from Davy Crockett's 1837 *Almanac of Wild Sports in the West*, and is entitled "A Desperate Contest with a Great Black Bear." Students may be familiar with the Davy Crockett of legend. In reality, Davy Crockett was a pioneer who served in the Tennessee legislature and the United States Congress. He died in Texas defending the Alamo against Mexico in 1836, just before the interior illustration was published. The almanacs he published contributed to the folklore of the wild American West.

INTERACTIVE ACTIVITY

Use the interactive tools to explore images from Davy Crockett's almanacs.

1. Look at the cover of Crockett's almanac, showing a man being attacked by a bear. Discuss what that indicates about life in the west.

2. Click the **Cartoon** tab to explore the cartoon from the Crockett Almanac showing "A Desperate Contest with a Great Black Bear." Have students use the **Magnifier** tool to examine the tools the people are using and the expressions on their faces, as well as that of the bear. Ask students to discuss who might win this contest. Also ask them to look for other signs of nature and wildlife, such as the fox clinging to the bear's leg.

3. Click the **Web Link** button to see the lyrics for "The Ballad of Davy Crockett."

TIPS

- Click the **Web Link** button and print and distribute the lyrics to "The Ballad of Davy Crockett." Play the instrumental music from the same link and let students sing along.

- Use the **Highlighter** tool to call attention to the motto "Go Ahead!!" on the Almanac cover. Ask students to discuss what the phrase suggests in the context of the Westward Movement.

Activity screen

A Pioneer Train Constitution: 1849

BACKGROUND INFORMATION

The Oregon Trail is the most famous of the trails pioneers carved out of the rugged landscape of the West. The trail began at Independence, Missouri (the jumping-off point), and followed the south bank of the Platte River, continued west through Nebraska, into Wyoming, and through the Rocky Mountains all the way to Oregon. The route was over 2,000 miles long.

Settlers were encouraged to take the trip by offers of free land from the United States government. More than 350,000 people made the arduous trip, one filled with hardship and peril, as evidenced in the diary excerpts.

The Pioneer Train Constitution of 1849 was written by the leaders of a wagon train. Groups often elected leaders to write such rules of conduct during the first weeks on the trail.

FEATURED INTERACTIVE ACTIVITY

Use this activity to explore a constitution written by leaders of a wagon train.

Purpose: Analyze the rules of conduct set forth for the travelers and make inferences about life on the trail.

1. Take turns reading the text of the Pioneer Train Constitution aloud, and ask students to discuss its meaning.

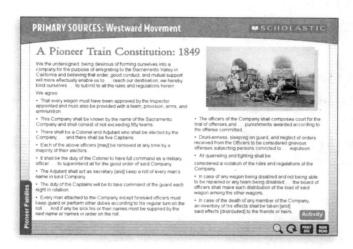

2. Click the **Activity** button to engage students in a multiple-choice activity. For the first question, read the brief excerpt from the Pioneer Train Constitution. Ask

students to infer the best meaning of the excerpt. You can take a show of hands, or have students write their answers down. Then click the **Reveal Answer** button to discover the correct answer. Move on to the next question by clicking the **Next** button, or selecting one of the numbered tabs on the left.

3. Allow students to make up their own restatements, as well, and record these with the **Pen** tool beside the list of answers.

4. Once they have carefully read the document, make sure students can identify the main goals of the Pioneer Train Constitution.

5. Click the **Pioneer Families** tab to see a photograph of the two families sitting by their wagons.

On the Trail: 1847–1849

INTERACTIVE ACTIVITY

Use the interactive tools to explore the photographs and diary entries of pioneers on the trail.

1. Click the **Diary Excerpts** tab to toggle between text and photograph. Have students take turns reading the text. Or, click the **Audio** button to listen to the entries read aloud.

2. Click the **Next** arrow to move to another diary excerpt and photograph from life on the trail.

TIPS

• Use the **Microphone** tool, if available, to record students reading the diary entries.

• Use the **Pen** tool to write captions for the photographs.

Activity screens

The Gold Rush: 1849

BACKGROUND INFORMATION

Soon after the first pioneers began their journeys, there was another strong lure out West—the discovery of gold by John Marshall at Sutter's Mill in 1848. In the years that

THE WAY THEY GO TO CALIFORNIA.

followed, thousands of people clamored to reach California from all over the world. It launched one of the greatest migrations of people in American history. In one single year, 1849, the population of California increased from 20,000 to more than 100,000. One group that contributed to the population boom was Chinese immigrants, who left their home country in large numbers because of a series of natural disasters and high taxes, and were lured to California by the promise of a "gold mountain." Chinese immigrants composed one fifth of the mining population by the end of the 1850s.

The trip was difficult, the camps were dangerous, and living conditions were incredibly expensive and occasionally violent. Some struck it rich. For many, however, the promises of wealth did not pan out.

FEATURED INTERACTIVE ACTIVITY

Use the activity to explore a cartoon about the Gold Rush.

Purpose: Draw conclusions about different perspectives on the Gold Rush during this period.

1. Look at the cartoon, "The Way They Go to California."

2. Click the **Photograph** tab to see European and Chinese immigrant workers laying tracks. Review the background information on Chinese immigration.

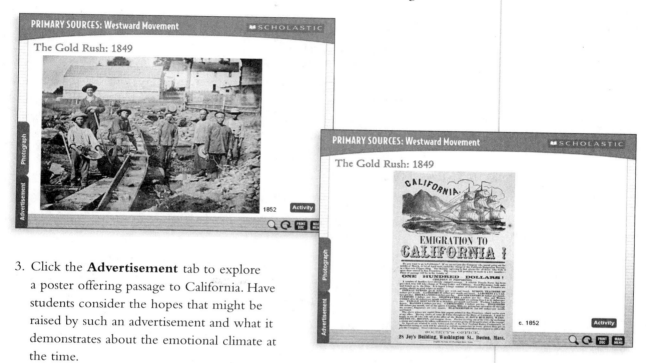

3. Click the **Advertisement** tab to explore a poster offering passage to California. Have students consider the hopes that might be raised by such an advertisement and what it demonstrates about the emotional climate at the time.

4. Return to the landing page and click the **Activity** button to explore the cartoon more thoroughly.

5. Point out the blank speech balloons on the cartoon.

6. Have students select which text on the right belongs in each speech balloon.

7. Have them drag the letter next to each quotation into the correct speech balloon.

8. Click the **Reveal Answers** button to see the correct placement of the speech balloons in the cartoon.

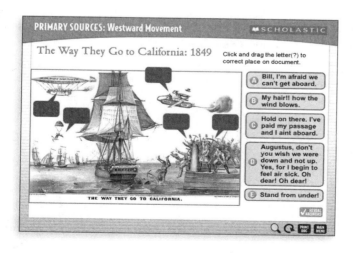

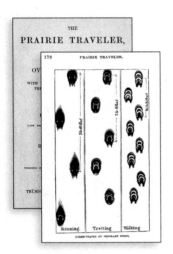

Activity screen

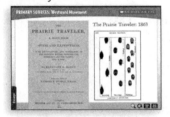

The Prairie Traveler

BACKGROUND INFORMATION

The wood engraving of horse tracks comes from a how-to guide for pioneers written by Randolph B. Marcy, called *The Prairie Traveler, a Hand-Book for Overland Expeditions* (the cover appears here, as well). The guide features maps and detailed descriptions of the major overland routes between Mississippi and the Pacific Ocean. It includes such tips as how to best pack a wagon and what to do in case of snakebite. This chart shows how a traveler can interpret a horse's hoof prints to determine the speed and type of horse.

INTERACTIVE ACTIVITY

Use the interactive tools to explore this handbook for overland explorers.

1. Look together at the cover for *The Prairie Traveler.*

2. Examine the page showing the horse tracks at different speeds.

3. Click the **Excerpt** tab and have a student read aloud the excerpt from the handbook. Ask students what they can imply about Marcy's view of "Indians" and the interactions he expects his readers to have with them.

TIPS

• Use the **Magnifier** tool to look at the hoof prints more closely.

• Use the **Print Doc** button to print out copies of the horse tracks chart. Ask students to calculate how many feet are represented in each column.

The Pony Express: 1860

BACKGROUND INFORMATION

Although the Pony Express is legendary, it was in existence for only 19 months. In March, 1860, the first rider took off on horse from St. Joseph, Missouri, with 49 letters and a newspaper. Using a rider-relay system, the mail reached Sacramento just ten days later, faster than with any system previously used.

The Pony Express captured people's imaginations and brought news from the "Golden State" of California closer. However, the advent of the telegraph (next activity) soon put the Pony Express out of business.

INTERACTIVE ACTIVITY

Use the interactive tools to explore a flyer advertising the Pony Express.

1. Look together at the announcement about the Pony Express.

2. Invite students to read the copy aloud. Have them notice references to speed in the image and words.

Activity screen

TIPS

- Refer back to the Map of the Westward Movement to locate Kansas and Sacramento, CA. Discuss how fast the rider would need to travel to cover 2,000 miles in ten days.

- Have students use the **Pen** tool to highlight parts of the text and illustration that indicate speed. Ask students what might be meant by "Clear the Track" on the poster.

The Overland Telegraph: 1861

BACKGROUND INFORMATION

The documents on this page show a key development in the history of communication. The telegraph was invented in 1844 by Samuel F. B. Morse, and the photograph shows the tape from the first message sent over telegraphic wires—from Washington, D.C., to Baltimore. The message reads "What hath God wrought?"
The words are encoded in dots and dashes embossed into the long tape by signals from electrical impulses.

The 1861 excerpt from *The New York Times* highlights the completion of the Overland Telegraph line, from New York to San Francisco. This accomplishment enabled the invention to be used to communicate across the country. It effectively put the Pony Express (see previous activity) out of business.

FEATURED INTERACTIVE ACTIVITY

Use the activity to explore the invention of the telegraph.

Purpose: Understand the impact of technology on the Westward Movement.

1. Look together at the newspaper article describing the completion of the telegraph line. Have students take turns reading the article aloud.

2. Look at an image of the first telegraph ever sent. Slide the **Pull** arrow to the left to see the complete telegraph.

3. Click the **Audio** button to hear the text of the telegraph, "What hath God wrought?" in Morse code.

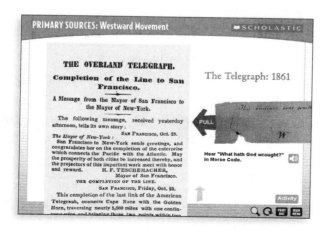

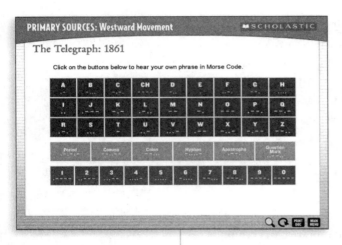

4. Click the **Activity** button to let students spell out their own phrases in Morse code.

5. Have students take turns clicking on different letters to spell a name, word, or phrase. Other students can try to listen and figure out what the words are.

6. Click the **Print Doc** button to print out charts for each student or small group to refer to while listening to or creating coded words.

Growth of the Railroad: 1860s

BACKGROUND INFORMATION

In 1862, President Abraham Lincoln signed a bill authorizing the construction of a transcontinental railroad. In 1863, two companies began building the railroad—one from Sacramento, California, going east and one from Omaha, Nebraska, heading west.

The task was monumental and made a huge impact on the surrounding environment and the people involved. The railroad construction blasted tunnels through mountains, while new rails and bridges interrupted animal habitats. The lands of Native Americans were violated, and buffalo were killed off. Many people suffered backbreaking toil, including Chinese and Irish laborers.

However, six years later, in 1869, the two lines met in a much-celebrated moment at Promontory, Utah. The joining of the two long lines of track was historic, symbolic, and an incredible development in transportation. The amount of time for the overland journey was reduced from five months to eight days.

Activity screens

INTERACTIVE ACTIVITY

Use the interactive tools to explore the development and impact of the railroads.

1. Look at the schedule for travel west by railroad.

2. Click the **Photograph** tab to see a picture of workers celebrating the completion of the transcontinental railroad at Promentory, Utah.

3. Click the **Golden Spike** tab to see the golden spike that was driven into the ground to unite the two rails. Note that this spike was later removed for posterity.

4. Read the inscription that was engraved on the golden spike.

5. Click the **Poster** tab to explore a poster advertising the grand opening of the railroad.

TIPS

- Use the **Magnifier** tool to examine the timetable more closely. Have students look at a U.S. map to compare the distances covered and times indicated between the timetable and modern-day train or bus schedules.

- Have students locate some of the places on the schedule on the Map of the Westward Movement and determine which railroad line the schedule is for.

- Use the **Pen** tool to have students write their own inscriptions for the Golden Spike.

American Progress: 1872

BACKGROUND INFORMATION

The painting shown is one of the most commonly used images to depict the Westward Movement. George Crofutt was a publisher of travel guidebooks, and he commissioned John Gast to create a painting to be used as an illustration for his Western guides. He dictated to Gast the specific elements to incorporate in the painting. After it was completed, he made thousands of prints for the readers of his travel series.

The painting, *American Progress*, symbolizes the many aspects of the Westward Movement, including what became known as *manifest destiny*. The floating figure, pointing westward, suggests the inevitability of America's expansion.

FEATURED INTERACTIVE ACTIVITY

Use the activity to explore a painting depicting the Westward Movement.

Purpose: Recognize symbolism represented in the painting and discuss its meaning.

1. Look at John Gast's painting, *American Progress*, together. Share background information about how it was commissioned, using the information provided above.

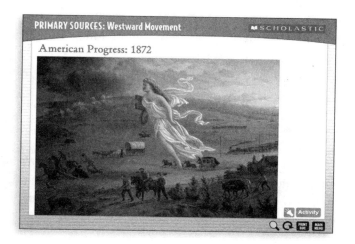

2. Click the **Spotlight** tool and look for symbols of Westward Movement and progress, such as wagons and telegraph lines.

3. Click the **Activity** button to explore the representations of East and West in the painting.

4. Pull the **East** tab on the right or the **West** tab on the left to reveal the two halves of the painting and have students use the **Pen** tool to fill in the chart, listing the symbols they see in the East and in the West. Discuss whose perspective is being represented.

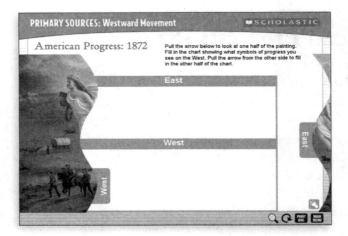

Glidden's Barbed Wire Patent: 1874

BACKGROUND INFORMATION

Barbed wire is an example of a seemingly minor invention—a mere twist of metal, it might appear—that changed the landscape of life in the West. Before the invention of barbed wire, fencing was extremely problematic. Animals easily broke plain wire fences. Wooden fences were expensive and lumber was in scarce supply (thus the sod houses on farms).

In the 1870s, various versions of barbed wire emerged and competed for patents. The most successful of these was Joseph Glidden's. He also developed machinery to mass-produce the wire, adding to its success and popularity.

No longer did cattle roam freely and cowboys lead cattle drives. Farms and other property became more private, resources were less available for common use, and range wars were waged. Many Native American groups, used to nomadic lifestyles, were negatively affected. In fact, they called barbed wire "the Devil's rope." Nostalgia for the open lands developed almost immediately, captured in Cole Porter's song "Don't Fence Me In."

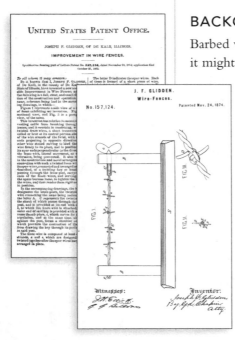

INTERACTIVE ACTIVITY

Use the interactive tools to explore the text and illustration for the patent for barbed wire.

1. Look at the application to the patent office for "improvement in wire fences."

2. Explore the illustration for barbed wire.

3. Use the background information to provide context for this important invention in Westward Movement.

Activity screen

TIPS

- Use the Westward Movement Time Line to put the barbed wire patent in historical context with the other developments of the Westward Movement.

- Use the **Magnifier** tool to read portions of the text of the patent. Direct students' attention to the third paragraph, which describes the purpose and advantages of the barbed wire design.

Life on the Frontier—Pioneers and Cowboys: Late 1800s

BACKGROUND INFORMATION

This collection of photographs offers several views of life for cowboys and pioneers of the American West.

The photographs were taken in the late 1800s. The houses were generally built out of the material most readily available—earth. Strips of sod were chopped into three-foot lengths and stacked in rows, like bricks. The houses that have wooden doors and glass windows reveal that the families living in them were among the more prosperous. The roofs of sod houses were covered with hay or brush, but most of them leaked when it rained.

Although the cowboys worked long, hard days, the photographs also reveal that they carried with them a sense of pride.

FEATURED INTERACTIVE ACTIVITY

Use the picture tour activity to explore daily life on the frontier.

Purpose: Analyze photographs to gain a deeper understanding of the quality of life for pioneers and cowboys on the frontier.

1. Look at the first screen showing photographs of pioneers and cowboys.

2. Click the **Picture Tour** button to look at slides from life on the frontier, and to listen to the narration

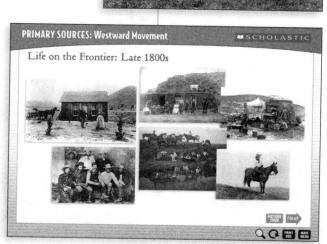

about the photographs. Use the **Pause** button at any point to stop and take a closer look at the photographs.

3. Click the **Next** button to see each full-sized image, read a short caption, and hear the extended audio narration.

PRIMARY SOURCES: Westward Movement — SCHOLASTIC

Life on the Frontier (Pioneers): Late 1800s

A cow grazes on the roof of a sod house in Nebraska.

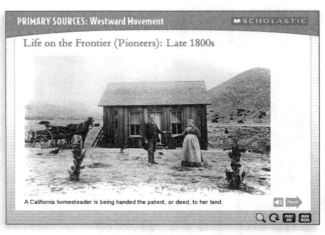

PRIMARY SOURCES: Westward Movement — SCHOLASTIC

Life on the Frontier (Pioneers): Late 1800s

A California homesteader is being handed the patent, or deed, to her land.

PRIMARY SOURCES: Westward Movement — SCHOLASTIC

Life on the Frontier (Cowboys): Late 1800s

Cowboys took a break on the range to bathe and relax.

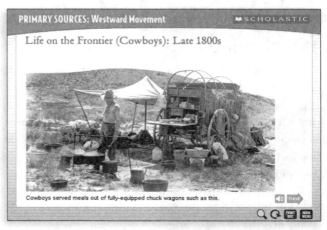

PRIMARY SOURCES: Westward Movement — SCHOLASTIC

Life on the Frontier (Cowboys): Late 1800s

Cowboys served meals out of fully-equipped chuck wagons such as this.

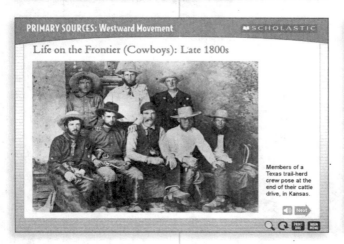

PRIMARY SOURCES: Westward Movement — SCHOLASTIC

Life on the Frontier (Cowboys): Late 1800s

Members of a Texas trail-herd crew pose at the end of their cattle drive, in Kansas.

PRIMARY SOURCES: Westward Movement — SCHOLASTIC

Life on the Frontier (Cowboys): Late 1800s

The romantic image of the west is captured in this photograph of a lone cowboy in the wide-open west.

The Wild West: 1890s

BACKGROUND INFORMATION

Perhaps nothing conveyed the exciting appeal of the Wild West better than Buffalo Bill's Wild West show, organized by William Cody in 1883 and performed for 30 years. The show featured bucking broncos, lassoing cowboys, and an international exhibition called the Congress of Rough Riders of the World.

The performers demonstrated roping, shooting, and riding skills, and portrayed tales of cowboys, Indians, the Pony Express, hunters, and cavalry scouts. These often-exaggerated portraits contributed to the romantic myth of life in the American West.

Performers included Annie Oakley, Buck Taylor, and even the Sioux chief, Sitting Bull (although he found it demeaning and quit after one season).

INTERACTIVE ACTIVITY

Use the interactive tools to explore a poster for Buffalo Bill's Wild West show.

1. Use the background information to provide context for the Wild West show. Look at the poster advertising "the show of shows" together.

2. Use the **Pull** arrow to move the poster to the left. Click the poster and drag right or left to see poster in its entirety.

3. Discuss what students can determine about the points of view shown in the poster toward the "Wild West" and toward Native Americans.

TIPS

Use the **Magnifier** tool to focus on different elements of the poster. Ask students to find different skills being demonstrated. Also look for images that romanticize the culture of the Wild West.

Use the **Highlighter** tool to point out the phrases that deal with light: *illuminated*; *lighter than day*; *25,000 candle power*. Also point out the indications of light in the background. Discuss why the lighting was so noteworthy.

Activity screen

Chief Joseph's Surrender Speech: 1877

BACKGROUND INFORMATION

Chief Joseph was the leader of the Nez Percé Indians who lived in the Wallowa Valley (in present-day Oregon, Idaho, and Washington).

In the early 1870s, the Nez Percé were engaged in a losing battle against the United States Army for their land. Chief Joseph was their leader, and he began to realize that they could not continue to fight. However, he did not want to surrender. He led a march to Canada in 1877.

The tribe successfully crossed the rugged terrain of Idaho and Montana (more than 1,000 miles) fighting off entanglements over a 15-week period. However, they were finally captured just 30 miles south of Canada's border. It was then that Chief Joseph gave this memorable speech. For the rest of his life, he petitioned for the Nez Percé people to be allowed to return to their homeland.

Activity screen

INTERACTIVE ACTIVITY

Use the interactive tools to explore the surrender speech given by Chief Joseph on behalf of the Nez Percé Indians.

1. Look at the painting of Chief Joseph by historical painter Robert Lindneux, circa 1940.

2. Use the background information to provide context for the speech.

3. Read the transcript of the speech together.

4. Click the **Audio** button to hear his speech read aloud.

TIPS

• Use the **Microphone** tool, if available, to let students read and record the speech themselves.

• Use the **Highlighter** tool to emphasize all the references to death in the speech. Discuss why death features so prominently in the surrender speech.

The Indian Territory: Late 1800s

BACKGROUND INFORMATION

In the 1830s and 1840s, 70,000 Native Americans in the Southeast were removed from their lands by the United States government and settled in the West in an area known as the Indian Territory (now Oklahoma). Their forced march became known as the Trail of Tears.

By the 1870s, the fertile land of the Indian Territory became desirable to white settlers. The advertisement shown here, encouraging settlers to move west, illustrates the climate of the time. Pioneers began encroaching, illegally, into the territory. Posters like the one shown were circulated throughout the West.

The engraving called "Killing Buffalo for Pleasure" shows another aspect of the impact of the white settlers on the Native Americans' way of life. The advent of the railroad had divided herds and brought in hunters. These hunters killed buffalo for sport and also to sell their hides for profit. But another, even more insidious, motive existed—to destroy the food supply for the Native Americans and make their land available for cattle drives and settlers.

The photograph of dead buffalo conveys the scope of the decimation of the Native Americans' way of life. The final two photographs show Native American groups forced to live in captivity.

INTERACTIVE ACTIVITY

Use the interactive tools to explore the advertisement, engraving, and photographs depicting the impact of the Westward Movement on Native Americans.

1. Look at the poster advertising the "Grand Rush for the Indian Territory!"

2. Use the background information to explain the Trail of Tears and the impact of the U.S. government's encroachment on the Indian Territory.

3. Click the **Next** arrow to look at an engraving showing "Killing Buffalo for Pleasure." Discuss the impact of this sport on Native Americans in the area. Also discuss the impact of the railroad itself on the buffalo.

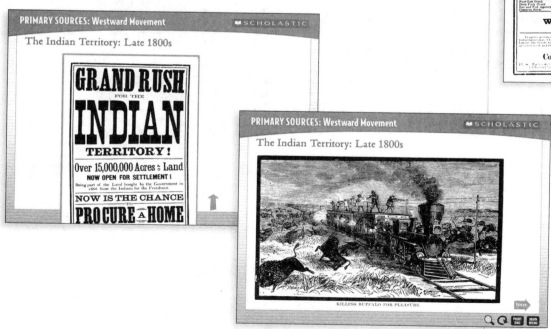

4. Click the **Next** arrow again to see a more graphic depiction of the affect on buffalo.

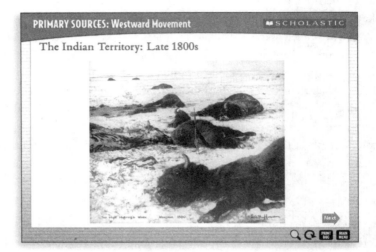

5. Click the **Next** arrows again to see two photographs of Native American groups being forced to live in captivity.

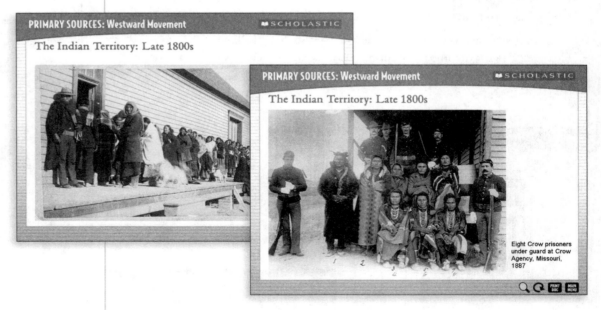

TIPS

• Use the **Magnifier** tool to zoom in on aspects of these documents for closer examination.

• Use the **Pen** tool to write captions for the photographs.

Civil War

OVERVIEW

The Civil War was the most divisive, destructive conflict in American history. More than 623,000 soldiers died on both sides. That is about the same number killed as in all other U.S. wars combined. Hundreds of thousands more were wounded. When it was over, much of the South lay in ruins.

The causes of the Civil War are varied, complex, and subject to bitter debate. For instance, saying that the Civil War was about slavery is not wrong, but it is incomplete. It was also about economics, class, and politics. These complexities present an opportunity to introduce your students to the idea that history is not clear-cut, even upon close examination.

Although the Civil War ended slavery, it did not end racism. Reconstruction was the beginning of a slow struggle that exploded, a century later, into the civil rights movement. And though the United States is much more integrated and heterogeneous than it was in the 1800s, racial and cultural issues continue to divide our people. We still wrestle with the legacy of the Civil War. The primary sources in this section will help explain why.

NOTE: The Civil War section is organized in two files on the CD: Part 1 and Part 2. The documents and activities for each are listed on the right.

Civil War Time Line (1850–1865)

1850
Congress passes the Fugitive Slave Act

1851
Harriet Beecher Stowe's best-selling novel *Uncle Tom's Cabin* is published

1857
The U.S. Supreme Court hands down its Dred Scott decision declaring that slaves and free blacks are not citizens

1859
Radical abolitionist John Brown leads an unsuccessful assault on the federal arsenal at Harpers Ferry, Virginia (now West Virginia)

November 6, 1860
Abraham Lincoln is elected president of the United States

December 20, 1860
South Carolina secedes from the Union

January–February 1861
Six more states secede—Mississippi, Florida, Alabama, Georgia, Louisiana, and Texas

February 9, 1861
Jefferson Davis is elected president of the Confederate States of America at a secession convention in Montgomery, Alabama

March 4, 1861
Lincoln is inaugurated

April 12, 1861
Confederate cannons open fire on federal troops in Fort Sumter, beginning the war

April–May, 1861
Four more southern states secede—Virginia, Arkansas, Tennessee, and North Carolina — expanding the Confederacy to 11 states

April 20, 1861
Col. Robert E. Lee of Virginia resigns from the U.S. Army; he later becomes the Confederacy's top general

May 1861
Escaped slaves are employed by Union forces for the first time and declared contraband (confiscated property) of war

November 1, 1861
Gen. George B. McClellan becomes the U.S. Army commander in chief

March 9, 1862
The world's first battle between ironclad ships takes place at Hampton Roads, Virginia; the fight between the Union's Monitor and the Confederacy's Merrimac (or Virginia) is a draw

September 17, 1862
The Union wins the battle of Antietam in Maryland

September 22, 1862
Lincoln announces that the Emancipation Proclamation, which frees slaves in the rebelling states, will go into effect January 1, 1863

May 4, 1863
Robert E. Lee wins his most decisive victory at Chancellorsville, Virginia, but loses his best general, Thomas "Stonewall" Jackson

July 1–3, 1863
The Union wins the three-day battle of Gettysburg in Pennsylvania

July 4, 1863
Confederate forces surrender to Grant at Vicksburg, Mississippi; the Union now controls the entire Mississippi River; losses at Gettysburg and Vicksburg stagger the South

November 19, 1863
Lincoln delivers the Gettysburg Address

March 9, 1864
Lincoln makes Grant the U.S. Army's top commander

September 2, 1864
Union General William T. Sherman takes Atlanta, a vital Confederate supply center

November 8, 1864
Lincoln is reelected

March 3, 1865
The Freedman's Bureau is established

March 4, 1865
Lincoln's second inauguration is held

April 3, 1865
The Confederate capital, Richmond, Virginia, falls to Union troops

April 9, 1865
Lee surrenders to Grant at Appomattox Court House in Virginia; the war is over

April 14, 1865
Lincoln is shot by actor John Wilkes Booth and dies the next day; Andrew Johnson is sworn in as president

December 18, 1865
The 13th Amendment to the Constitution, which abolishes all slavery, goes into effect.

TEACHING NOTES

Civil War Time Line

FEATURED INTERACTIVE ACTIVITY

Use this interactive time line to preview milestones of the Civil War. Return to it to provide context for documents as you explore the primary sources in this collection.

Click the dots to read about key events of the Civil War. To add your own event, drag a bubble shape from the **Add Event** button to the time line and use the **Pen** or **On-screen Keyboard** tool to write in a description.

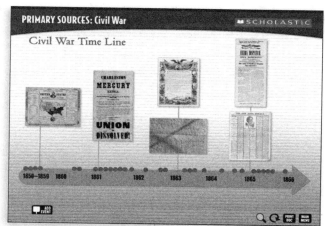

Map of the Civil War

FEATURED INTERACTIVE ACTIVITY

Use this map activity to explore the location of key places during the Civil War. Return to the map as you explore the primary sources to provide geographic context for each document.

Map 1: States of the Civil War Period

1. Drag each state abbreviation from the chart on the right to the correct place on the map.

2. Click **Reveal Answers** to check the answers or to see the map filled in without completing the activity.

3. Click the **Next** arrow to explore Map 2.

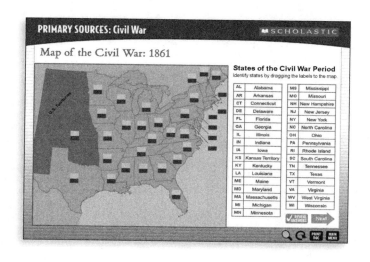

See page 93 for a reproducible map activity sheet. Answer Key, page 94.

Map 2: Union and Confederate States

1. Have students choose whether each state was part of the Union or Confederacy by selecting the blue or gray dots in the chart.

2. Click **Reveal Answers** to check the answers or to see the map filled in without completing the activity.

3. Click the **Next** arrow to explore Map 3.

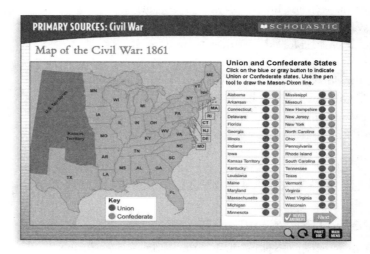

Map 3: Key Battles

1. Have students drag the name of the battle into the space on the map where the battle occurred. Correct placements will stick; incorrect placements will bounce back.

2. Click the **Reveal Years** button to see when each battle took place.

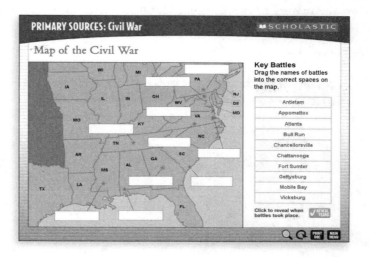

Slaves for Sale: 1850s–1860s

BACKGROUND INFORMATION

Pictured here are tags assigned to enslaved people of African descent in Charleston, South Carolina. The tags were worn by those who were rented by their owners to other employers. Each tag listed the enslaved person's number, skill (e.g., porter, servant, mechanic), and the year in which the tag was issued. After 1848, free blacks in Charleston also had to wear tags showing their status. Tags were used only in the Charleston area. Other marks of slave ownership, including branding, were frequently used in the South.

Broadsides were large sheets of paper used as news articles, announcements, or advertisements. This broadside announces an auction prompted by a slave owner's death. The price for each slave was determined by age, gender, skill, and the number of his or her physical infirmities. The price also took into account what the owner paid for him or her originally. At the bottom of the poster, the statement "Slaves will be sold separate, or in lots, as best suits the purchaser," indicates a willingness by the owner's heirs to split up slave families. Posters like this were common in the South.

INTERACTIVE ACTIVITY

Use the interactive tools to explore these artifacts of slavery, including slave tags and a slave auction broadside.

1. Look at the Slaves for Sale artifacts together and discuss what they reveal about how slaves were treated.

2. Click the **Slave Tags** tab to examine the tags more closely and to share the background information above.

3. Click the **Slave Auction** tab to explore a notice listing a deceased slave owner's slaves. Point out the notes made under "Qualification." Share that slaves were often sold individually to slave owners looking for people with specific skills. Ask students to infer what that meant for families, which are listed in groups here.

TIPS

• Use the **Magnifier** tool to examine the slave tags closely. Have students identify the location, identification number, name, and year on both tags.

• Use the **Magnifier** and **Highlighter** tools to explore the relationship of age to price listed. Look at the qualifications and explore how they relate to the price as well.

Activity screen

65

Political Chart of the United States: 1856

BACKGROUND INFORMATION

From the beginning, many people in the United States were convinced that slavery was wrong, and they fought to abolish it. By the 1850s, this issue had begun to divide the country.

This chart, featuring Republican presidential candidate John C. Frémont, illustrates many of the differences between the North and the South in the antebellum era. The Republican Party was founded in 1854, in direct response to the tensions produced by slavery. The Republican Party specifically favored banning the spread of slavery into the territories, a view held by many northerners. In fact, one Republican slogan rallied "Free Speech, Free Press, Free Soil, Free Men, Frémont, and Victory!" Democrats countered that Frémont would cause the southern states to secede. Though he lost the 1856 presidential election to James Buchanan, Frémont won 45 percent of the northern vote total, quite an accomplishment for a political party that was only two years old—and an indication that a significant number of people, especially in the North, were opposed to slavery.

Activity screen

INTERACTIVE ACTIVITY

Use the interactive tools to explore the differences between the North and the South as exhibited in this political chart.

1. Look at the political chart together and share the background information on the divisive issue of slavery.

2. Point out that this chart was produced for the Republican presidential candidate, John C. Frémont, and discuss how that might influence the presentation of facts.

3. Refer back to the Civil War Time Line to place this chart in the historical context of the antebellum (prewar) era.

4. Ask students if they can determine what Frémont's position on slavery was.

TIPS

- Use the **Magnifier** tool to zoom in on each section of the chart.

- Create a North/South T-chart and use the **Pen** tool to take notes about the facts presented for each side.

Cornerstone of the Confederacy: 1861

BACKGROUND INFORMATION

On December 20, 1860, South Carolina seceded from the Union. The Charleston Mercury broadside shows the announcement of the official ordinance dissolving the Union.

In February 1861, the Confederacy's Provincial Congress elected Alexander H. Stephens of Georgia as its vice president. Stephens' Cornerstone Speech was delivered at the Athenaeum in Savannah, Georgia, on March 21, 1861. Georgia and several other states had seceded, but the shelling of Fort Sumter was still about three weeks away.

According to the Savannah Republican, Stephens' Cornerstone speech was interrupted by cheering and applause several times. The newspaper reported that after the speech "Mr. Stephens took his seat, amid a burst of enthusiasm and applause, such as the Athenaeum has never had displayed within its walls, within 'the recollection of the oldest inhabitant.'"

In the speech, Stephens acknowledged clearly that slavery was the central tenet of the Confederacy. However, after the war, many southerners vigorously asserted that disagreements over states' rights, not slavery, had been the main cause for secession. Ironically, Stephens himself was one of the first to make the revisionist states' rights argument following the war.

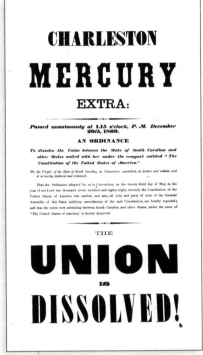

INTERACTIVE ACTIVITY

Use the interactive tools to explore these documents showing the origin of the Confederacy.

1. Look at the broadside announcing the secession of South Carolina from the Union, noting the date.

2. Click the **Confederate Speech** tab to read the speech that Alexander H. Stephens, the Confederacy's elected vice president, gave in March 1861.

3. Click the **Web Link** button to read Stephens' entire speech.

TIPS

- Use the **Magnifier** tool to read the text of the Charleston Mercury broadside.

- **Highlight** the facts presented in the broadside that answer the *Who, What, When, Where,* and *Why* questions addressed in news articles.

- Use the **Microphone** tool, if available, to record students reading parts of the speech.

Activity screens

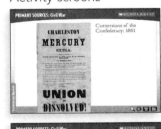

Songs of the War: 1860s

BACKGROUND INFORMATION

"Dixie's Land" became a popular hit shortly after being written by Ohioan Daniel D. Emmett in 1859. Different versions were sung by soldiers of both the North and the South, but it is the song most often associated with the South. While not an official anthem, it was played at Jefferson Davis's inaugural in 1861 and became a battle hymn for Southern troops. Although President Lincoln asked a band at the White House to play "Dixie" after the Confederate Army's surrender in 1865, the song remains closely associated with the Confederacy, and the word Dixie is still shorthand for the southern United States.

The origin of Dixie remains a mystery. One of the best explanations is that it originated in Louisiana, where a bank once printed $10 bills with the French word dix, or ten, on them. People supposedly called them "dixies," and Louisiana became known as "Dix's land." The name eventually encompassed the whole South. Years after the war, the song became controversial because of the romanticized view it portrayed of the cotton-picking life of a slave and because of the use of racist terms.

The story of "The Battle Hymn of the Republic" is more straightforward. One morning in 1861, Julia Ward Howe woke before dawn and quickly scrawled out a poem that had come to her. "The Battle Hymn of the Republic" was printed in the *Atlantic Monthly* the following February. At first, it seemed to be ignored. But then Union soldiers in the camps began singing it to the tune of the already popular "Glory, Hallelujah." The original sheet music and lyrics are both shown here. "The Battle Hymn of the Republic" became enormously popular—the most important song out of the hundreds written during the war. It remains a patriotic favorite.

FEATURED INTERACTIVE ACTIVITY

Use this activity to explore the sheet music and lyrics of Civil War songs.

Purpose: Compare and contrast the songs of the North and the South to analyze the role of music in the Civil War.

1. Look at the lyrics and sheet music together. Point out that the "Battle Hymn of the Republic" was written as a rallying cry for the Union and that "Dixie's Land" became an unofficial anthem of the South.

2. Use the background information above to provide context for each song, pointing out that music is often a fluid art form.

3. Click the **South** tab to see the sheet music cover for "Dixie's Land." Click the **Lyrics** button to read the lyrics, and press the **Audio** button to hear an instrumental recording.

4. Click the **North** tab to see the sheet music for "Battle Hymn of the Republic." Click the **Lyrics** button to read the lyrics. Point out that "Glory, Hallelujah" was a popular song in Union Army camps. Julia Ward Howe visited a Union Army camp and heard the soldiers singing the song, about John Brown's body. She was inspired to write her own lyrics, which became the "Battle Hymn of the Republic." Click the **Audio** button to hear Julia Ward Howe's song.

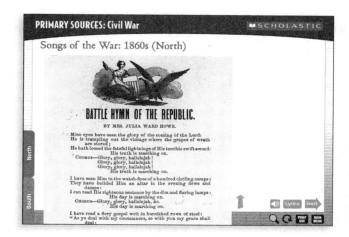

5. Return to the first screen of **Songs of the War**, and tell students that both sides adopted and created different versions of each song, which was typical for this era. Click the **Activity** button to explore two different versions of "Dixie's Land."

6. As students read the lyrics of the two "Dixie's Land" adaptations, have them infer which was created by the South and which by the North.

7. Invite students to label the two different versions with their guesses. Then click the **Reveal Answer** buttons to check their answers.

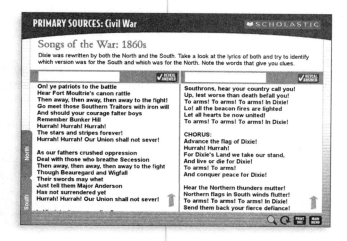

Wartime Photography: 1861–1864

BACKGROUND INFORMATION

The Civil War quickly became the most photographed war in history. That's not surprising because the art of photography was still young in 1861. The first working systems of photography were not developed until the early 1840s. Cameras of the time had extremely slow shutter speeds. Some took as long as 30 seconds to snap one picture. If the subject moved at all during that time, the camera would record a blur.

"Collodian" photography was the most common type during the war. To make a picture, a photographer had to coat the plate with expensive chemicals, expose it, and develop it all within a few minutes. It was tricky, but many found ingenious ways to rig up darkrooms on wagons and in shacks or cabins—and, despite all the difficulties, take beautiful, unforgettable images.

Most wartime photographers—including the best known, Mathew Brady—hailed from the North. Brady was nearly blind by then and took few photographs himself. But he hired a stable of talented photographers whose works were published under his name. After the war, some believed wrongly that Brady was the North's only photographer. Also, many people on both sides mistakenly believed that the South had no photographers of its own.

These documents show four images taken by photographers from both sides. Each picture captures war in a way not possible before photography.

FEATURED INTERACTIVE ACTIVITY

Use this Picture Tour to explore photographs from the Civil War era.

Purpose: Recognize the importance of the evolving technology of photography in documenting the Civil War.

1. Click the **Picture Tour** button to show a set of photographs with audio narration.

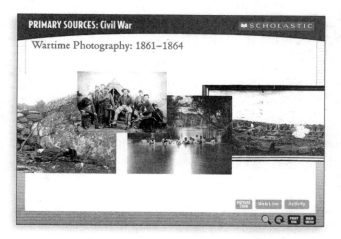

2. Click the **Activity** button to examine each photograph from the slide show individually.

3. Each photograph has a question on the side designed to encourage careful examination and analysis of the photograph. Have students use the **Pen** tool to record their answers. Or use the **Print Doc** button to let students record their answers on paper individually or in small groups.

4. Click the **Audio** button on each page to hear the narration for that particular slide.

5. Use the **Spotlight** tool to focus on different elements of the photographs, such as blurred figures that show motion, the soldiers in the left corner of the Fort Sumter battlefield, and the expressions on soldiers' faces.

6. Explore the photographs of the famous Civil War photographer, Matthew Brady, using the **Web Link** button.

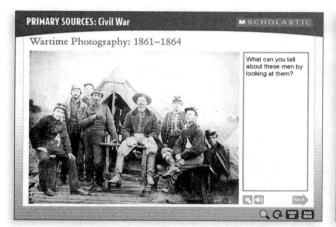

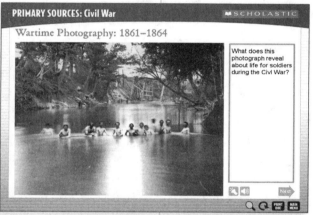

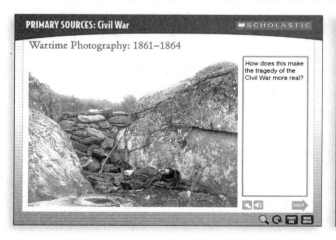

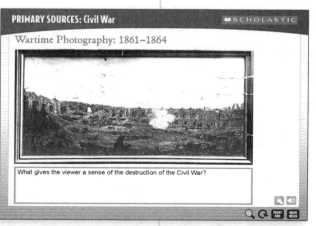

Letters Home About Soldier Life: 1864

BACKGROUND INFORMATION

Soldiers on both sides in the Civil War lived for the arrival of letters from home. One Union officer in Virginia wrote in March of 1865, "We have received no mail for several days and do not like it. A soldier can do without hard bread but not without his letters from home." When they had the time, supplies, and education, soldiers were prolific letter writers. Many of their letters were eloquent. Most carried requests for things like food, clothing, and more news from home. Many tried to convey to their friends and family what a soldier's life was like.

Here we have excerpts from two such letters—one Union, one Confederate. Spelling and punctuation have been altered somewhat for clarity.

INTERACTIVE ACTIVITY

Use the interactive tools to explore letters written by soldiers on both sides of the Civil War.

1. Look at the photographs of a Union soldier and a Confederate soldier. Note that the Confederate soldier, Lt. (John) Wallace Comer, is seated with his "body servant" standing at his side.

2. Click the **Letter** tabs to read the two different letters. Click the **Audio** buttons to hear the letters read aloud.

3. Compare and contrast what students glean about life for the two different soldiers.

TIPS

- Record students reading parts of the report using the **Microphone** tool, if available.

- Insert a new page and have students use the **Pen** tool to write their own replies to the soldiers.

- Use the **Magnifier** tool to zoom in on the photographs and examine what they reveal about soldiers' lives.

- Click the **Audio** button to hear the letters read aloud.

Activity screens

Hospitals and the Wounded:
Clara Barton: 1864

BACKGROUND INFORMATION

"Of all things, I'm going to avoid hospitals," one Union officer from Illinois wrote home early in the war. "They are far more dangerous than shot and shell." He spoke for every soldier North and South. Civil War doctors still did not understand the importance of sanitation in preventing infection and illness. They performed surgery and did their rounds in dirty, infected street clothes that spread disease. At a time when civilian hospitals were widely considered death houses, wartime hospitals could be hellish. According to one accounting, 67,000 Union soldiers died in action, but 43,000 died of wounds, and 224,000 died of disease. There are no reliable figures for the Confederacy.

Army officers frequently neglected their wounded, considering it unmilitary to fuss over injured soldiers. On the other hand, many doctors, nurses, officers, and ordinary people on both sides made heroic efforts to help the sick and wounded. Clara Barton began the war as a clerk in the U.S. Patent Office. Her concern for injured soldiers soon made her a one-woman medical corps that was never formally associated with the military or any group.

After the Battle of the Wilderness in early May 1864, Barton witnessed a typical display of military callousness toward the wounded and brought the complaint directly to a U.S. senator who pressured the War Department into action. A Union officer had refused to impose on the people of Fredericksburg, Virginia, by compelling them to house what he called "dirty, lousy, common soldiers"—his own men. Barton explained the results in her diary, which is excerpted here. Her description of the wounded men's plight is echoed in hundreds of accounts from other people on both sides of the fighting. Unfortunately, few of those accounts had such happy endings. After the war, Barton went on to found the American Red Cross in 1881.

Activity screens

INTERACTIVE ACTIVITY

Use the interactive tools to explore the contributions of Clara Barton to the Civil War.

1. Look at the photograph, which shows soldiers with a nurse receiving medical care on the battlefield.

2. Click the **Diary Excerpt** tab to read an entry from Clara Barton's diary, describing the plight of wounded soldiers on the battlefield.

3. Discuss the state of medical care during the Civil War and point out that there was much that doctors did not yet know about how to treat diseases and infection.

TIPS

- Use the **Magnifier** tool to zoom in on parts of the photograph. Ask students to look for details that reveal aspects of medical care at the time.

- Use the **Highlighter** tool to indicate phrases in the diary entry that also provide details about medical conditions.

- Use the **Microphone** tool, if available, to record students reading parts of the diary.

Civil War Submarine: CSS *H. L. Hunley*: 1864

BACKGROUND INFORMATION

The Civil War saw many technological firsts. It was the first war in which the telegraph played a key role, the first in which large numbers of troops were moved by train, the first in which land mines were used, and the first to witness a clash of ironclad ships.

On February 17, 1864, the Civil War introduced another first: the first submarine to sink an enemy ship. The Confederate sub CSS *H. L. Hunley* rammed the wooden

ship USS *Housatonic* just outside of Charleston Harbor in South Carolina. On the *Hunley's* ram was a long pole with a 135-pound explosive device attached. Having stuck the bomb on the hull of the *Housatonic*, the *Hunley* pulled back. As it did so, the bomb went off. The Union ship sank in three minutes, killing five sailors.

The *Hunley* attacked the *Housatonic* in a failed effort to break the Federal blockade that was starving the South of badly needed food, guns, and other supplies from Europe. However, its mission was a desperate one. The *Hunley* was basically a long metal tube powered by the frantic hand-cranking of eight men. Previously, the sub had sunk twice, killing both crews. On the night it sank the *Housatonic*, the *Hunley* shined a blue light toward Charleston, signaling a successful mission. Then the sub disappeared.

The mystery of the *Hunley* was finally solved in 1995, when an underwater search team found the sub's wreck. It was lifted from 30 feet of water in 2000 and excavated. In the wreckage, researchers discovered a U.S. $20 gold coin (right) that had been carried by the *Hunley's* last commander, Lt. George Dixon. According to family lore, a girlfriend had given Dixon the coin as a good-luck piece. While fighting at the battle of Shiloh, the coin turned out to be lucky indeed. It deflected a Yankee bullet fired at point-blank range.

After Shiloh, Dixon had the dented coin inscribed:

Shiloh
April 6, 1862
My life Preserver
G.E.D.

INTERACTIVE ACTIVITY

Use the interactive tools to explore the development of technology during the Civil War.

1. Look at the painting of the *Hunley* together. Give students some background about the invention of the submarine and the battle between the *Hunley* and the *Housatonic*, using the background information above.

2. Click the **Web Link** button to learn more about the *Hunley* and about this particular painting by Conrad Wise Chapman.

3. Click the **Gold Coin Artifact** tab to look at a coin that was discovered when the *Hunley* was found and excavated. Share the story about the coin's history provided in the background information.

Activity screens

TIPS

• Use the **Magnifier** tool to explore the painting of the submarine. Ask students how safe they think this submarine from the 1860s might have been and how it compares to submarines today.

• Use the **Pen** tool to write speech bubbles that correspond to the figures in the painting. What might they be saying to each other?

• Use the **Magnifier** tool to examine both sides of the gold coin artifact.

• Use the **Pen** tool to let students write a caption that describes the significance of the coin.

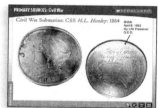

Emancipation Proclamation: 1863

BACKGROUND INFORMATION

Early on, Abraham Lincoln was reluctant to frame the Civil War as a crusade to free slaves, in part because he did not think he could legally take away property that was granted by the Constitution. Also, he did not want to push the four loyal, slave-holding border states—Delaware, Maryland, Kentucky, and Missouri—into the Confederacy's arms.

But his perspective changed as the war dragged on and most Northerners began to acknowledge slavery as its root cause. Also, Lincoln saw that many freed slaves wanted to serve as Union soldiers. Most important, the South's hopes hinged on winning recognition and help from England and France. Both countries wanted the South's cotton but opposed slavery. If Lincoln made freeing the South's slaves one of his war aims, neither European power would dare recognize the Confederacy.

On advice from Secretary of State William Seward, Lincoln withheld announcing the Emancipation Proclamation until the Union had scored a convincing victory. That came on September 17, 1862, at the Battle of Antietam. Five days later, Lincoln warned that slaves would be freed in all states, or parts of states, that were still in rebellion on January 1, 1863. The border states would not be affected. When that day arrived, Lincoln made good on his threat. The proclamation led to the passing of the 13th Amendment to the Constitution in 1865, which ended slavery throughout the United States.

The broadside, a northern publication, features the text of the proclamation framed by accompanying illustrations depicting the fruits of justice brought about by the end of slavery in the South. The political cartoon describes Lincoln, surrounded by symbols of evil and an image of a slave revolt, writing the Emancipation Proclamation. The cartoon presents the view of many Southerners at the time that the proclamation would cause social chaos and destruction.

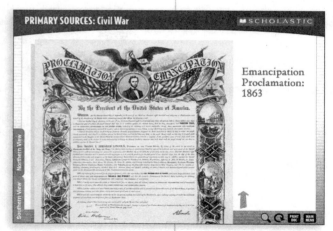

Emancipation Proclamation: 1863

FEATURED INTERACTIVE ACTIVITY

Use this activity to explore Lincoln's famous document declaring the abolishment of slavery.

Purpose: Examine the Emancipation Proclamation from multiple perspectives.

1. Look at the printed version of the Emancipation Proclamation together, which was printed in a northern publication. Point out the art around the margins.

2. Click the **Northern View** tab. Before clicking the **Audio** button, tell students to listen for the recurring words "free" and "freedom." As you play the recording, invite a student to click the plus sign on the **Freedom Counter** every time the class notices these words.

3. To read a transcript of part of the proclamation, click the **Excerpt** button.

4. Click the **Activity** button. Tell students that the images on the right are the medallions that appear as border art on the proclamation. Three of these medallions depict life before emancipation and three show life after. Have students drag the images to the correct column. Images placed in the correct column will stick; images placed incorrectly will bounce back.

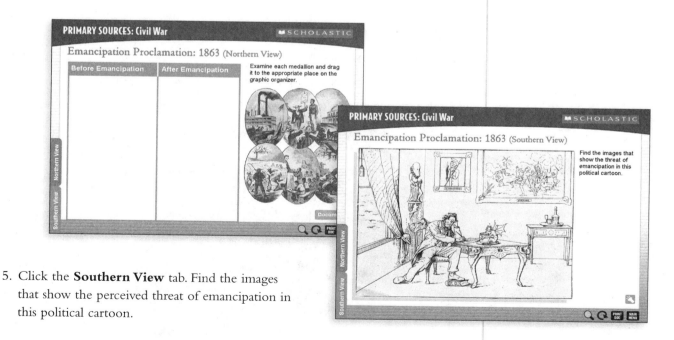

5. Click the **Southern View** tab. Find the images that show the perceived threat of emancipation in this political cartoon.

Gettysburg Address: 1863

BACKGROUND INFORMATION

Only two minutes in length, the Gettysburg Address is a cornerstone document in American history. Abraham Lincoln delivered it November 19, 1863, at ceremonies dedicating the cemetery at the Gettysburg battlefield. The speech reflects Lincoln's changing thinking about the meaning of the Civil War. As historian James M. McPherson points out, Lincoln's early speeches describe the United States as a "Union." But in the Gettysburg Address the word "union" never appears. Instead, Lincoln uses the word "nation." The Gettysburg Address signals the moment that the U.S. went from being a loose aggregate of states to becoming a unified country.

Lincoln wrote five versions of the Gettysburg Address. He revised the speech even as he delivered it. For instance, the written speech he carried did not contain the phrase, "under God." As a result, there is some controversy about exactly which version Lincoln delivered. However, the fifth version is the only one he signed his name to, and it is believed to be the most authentic.

There was some criticism of Lincoln's speech at the time. But many people recognized its brilliance right away. Several newspapers praised it. Edward Everett, the main speaker at the dedication ceremony, wrote to Lincoln: "I should be glad if I could flatter myself that I came as near to the central idea of the occasion in two hours as you did in two minutes."

FEATURED INTERACTIVE ACTIVITY

Use this activity to explore the famous speech given at the Gettysburg battleground.

Purpose: Study the language and meaning behind Lincoln's words.

1. Look at the document together.

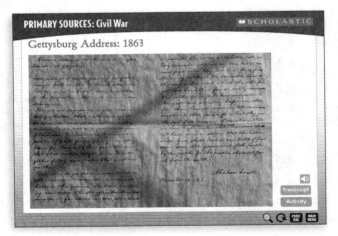

2. Click the **Audio** button to listen to the speech aloud. To highlight the brevity of the speech, have students time the length of the recording. (It lasts just under 2 minutes.)

3. Click the **Transcript** button to read the text. Allow students to use the **Microphone** tool, if available, to record themselves reading the speech.

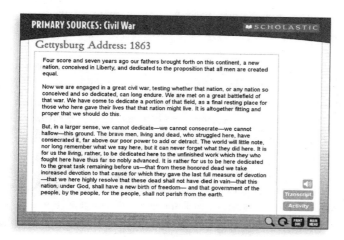

4. Click the **Activity** button to read a set of multiple-choice questions. For each statement from the Gettysburg Address, have students pick the answer that restates it best. Click the **Reveal Answer** button to check their answers.

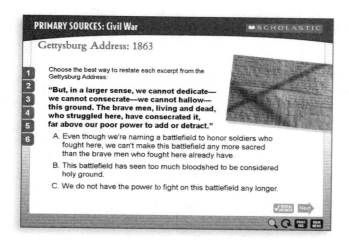

Activity screens

Contrabands: Early 1860s

BACKGROUND INFORMATION

Almost as soon as Union troops marched into the South, they were besieged by runaway slaves. This was a problem because the war was officially being fought solely to preserve the Union, not to end slavery. As a result, many escaped slaves were forcibly returned to Confederate owners by Union soldiers.

By early 1862, though, many Union officers began giving shelter to slaves. Many of these slaves were put to work for the army as spies, scouts, laborers, and cooks. In late 1862, a few abolitionist officers formed experimental volunteer regiments made up of former slaves. Such enlistment was illegal, or "contraband."

The recruiting of black soldiers became official in 1863 with Lincoln's Emancipation Proclamation. Blacks served in segregated units commanded by white officers. They received poorer medical attention and lower pay than whites. (The pay issue was finally remedied retroactively by Congress.) And if captured, black soldiers could expect to be killed or sold into slavery, though not all were. Nevertheless, by war's end, nearly 179,000 African Americans had enlisted and about 40,000 had died in service. The group photograph on this page shows the Band of 107th U.S. Colored Infantry at Fort Corcoran, taken in Arlington, Virginia, in 1865.

This section also highlights a contraband boy called Jackson. These two photos show his dramatic transformation from contraband to drummer boy for the 79th U.S. Colored Troops in Louisiana. We can sketch out some of the details of his life in the army: A drummer boy's main job was to keep a steady beat so that his unit could march in time. In camp, drummer boys carried water, took care of horses, ran errands, carried messages, and even cooked. During battles, they worked in hospitals, fetched ammunition, carried wounded and dead soldiers, and often became soldiers themselves.

INTERACTIVE ACTIVITY

Use the interactive tools to explore these photographs of escaped slaves who became soldiers.

1. Look at the photograph of a contraband drummer as well as the 107th Colored Infantry.

2. Explain that the term "contrabands" referred to escaped slaves who fled to and enlisted with Union forces. (Such enlistment was illegal or *contraband*.)

3. Explore the before and after photographs of Jackson. Discuss the changes in his appearance and life between the two photographs.

4. Examine the photograph of the Colored Infantry. Share with students the background information above and ask them to discuss details they notice in the photograph.

TIPS

- Use the **Magnifier** tool to explore the three photographs in more detail.
- Use the **Pen** tool to let students write captions for the photographs.

"Saved Colors:" 1864

BACKGROUND INFORMATION

On September 29, 1864, Sergeant-Major Christian Fleetwood of the 4th U.S. Colored Troops (USCT) put in his diary a three-sentence account of a battle he'd just fought in. Of his own actions, he wrote simply, "Saved colors." What he meant was that he had saved his regiment's colors from capture by the enemy. Fleetwood did not say exactly how he had done this until decades later, when he wrote a fuller description reprinted in part here. His actions that day won the attention of his superiors and a Medal of Honor—America's highest military award.

Fleetwood's memoir describes his role in the battle of Chaffin's Farm (or New Market Heights) near Richmond, Virginia. By the time that two-day battle was fought, African-American soldiers were a common sight in the Union Army. Thirteen black regiments fought at Chaffin's Farm, a Union victory. Of the 16 Medal of Honor decorations won by black soldiers in the war, 14 of them came from this one battle.

Few soldiers serving in the USCT wrote down their experiences, probably because the literacy among them was low. Fleetwood, just 23 at the time of the battle, was unusual in that he was born a free man (in Baltimore) and later graduated from college. His experiences at Chaffin's Farm were harrowing, and yet most combat veterans on either side could have related many similar tales.

Union regiments carried a pair of flags, or colors—a U.S. flag and a special regimental flag. Soldiers from the North and the South were encouraged to invest themselves emotionally in their colors. A unit that lost its colors to the enemy was humiliated. Being a color bearer was a high honor, but likely to be a brief one. A color bearer's prominence in battle made him an easy target.

INTERACTIVE ACTIVITY

Use the interactive tools to explore Sergeant-Major Fleetwood's account of saving his regiment's flags from a battleground.

1. Look at the photograph and provide background information about Fleetwood and the Battle of Chaffin's Farm.

2. Discuss the meaning of "saving the colors" (see background information above) and read aloud the introduction to Fleetwood's account.

3. Note that Fleetwood won a Medal of Honor for his actions. Invite students to discuss why he was bestowed this high military award.

TIP

- Use the **Microphone** tool, if available, to let students read and record Fleetwood's diary entry.

Activity screens

Activity screens

"Diary of a Georgia Girl": 1864

BACKGROUND INFORMATION

After capturing and destroying Atlanta, Union General William T. Sherman embarked on the boldest, most controversial attack of the Civil War. Starting on November 16, 1864, he marched his army through Georgia's barely defended heartland in an effort to destroy the South's food, supplies, and will to fight. "If the North can march an army right through the South," he wired his friend and commander, Ulysses S. Grant, "it is proof positive that the North can prevail."

The South had only a 10,000-man force to face Sherman's 62,000-man army. A few Confederates tried to make a stand, but Sherman simply went around or destroyed them. However, Sherman's aim was not to kill people—neither soldiers nor civilians. He wanted to destroy property that might give aid and comfort to Confederates. At this, Sherman's soldiers succeeded brilliantly. For most of them, "Sherman's March" became a rampage in which they took or demolished as much as they pleased.

Despite Southern atrocity stories, very few civilians were killed or hurt outright by Sherman's troops. Those who were killed or hurt were generally victims of Southern looters or Union "bummers"—renegades from Sherman's army. However, this was small comfort to the civilians in Sherman's path who watched their homes, valuables, and livestock brazenly destroyed or carried off. As one of Sherman's aides put it, "It is a terrible thing to see the terror and grief of these women and children."

The impotent rage Southerners felt toward Sherman is reflected in the diary of Eliza Andrews, a 24-year-old judge's daughter from Washington, Georgia. Though her own home was not directly affected, Andrews saw firsthand the miles of wasteland that the Union army left behind. The drawing shows Sherman's soldiers at work tearing up the Georgia countryside.

INTERACTIVE ACTIVITY

Use the interactive tools to explore a young Georgia woman's perspective on the aftermath of Sherman's march.

1. Provide some background about Sherman's march, using the background information above.

2. Click the **Drawing** tab to look at a drawing of the destruction that occurred during Sherman's march, shown from a Southern perspective.

3. Look at the picture of Eliza Andrews, and read the text of her diary entry. Click the **Audio** button to listen to the excerpt aloud.

4. Click the **Web Link** button to read more of Eliza Andrews' diary.

TIPS

- Use the **Spotlight** tool, if available, to examine the illustration, looking for evidence of destruction.

- Use the **Magnifier** to zoom in on the expressions on people's faces.

- Using the **Microphone** tool, if available, record further excerpts from the online version of Andrews' diary.

Bill Arp Philosophizes Upon the War, Etc.: 1864

BACKGROUND INFORMATION

Bill Arp was the pen name for Charles Henry Smith (1826–1903), a writer and politician from Rome, Georgia. Smith fought as a major for the Confederate Army until receiving a medical discharge in 1863. He became famous for his Bill Arp letters, which were reprinted in newspapers throughout the South. Though Smith had a college degree, a rare and expensive accomplishment at the time, the Arp letters were written as if they were spoken by a poor Southern farmer or backwoodsman.

Arp's homespun humor made him the South's unofficial jester. After the war, the editor of the Atlanta Constitution said that he doubted "if any papers ever produced a more thorough sensation than did the letters written by Major Smith during the war."

Indeed, Arp was a star of Southern journalism during the war. A typical newspaper at the time was made up of one to four pages that either used a four- or eight-column format. In a four-page paper, the front page was for big news, the second page for editorials and letters like Arp's, the third and fourth pages contained ads and miscellaneous minor news stories. Because literacy was so low in the South, news stories and features like the Arp letters were often read aloud, sometimes before mass gatherings.

Reprinted here are passages from a Bill Arp letter entitled "Bill Arp Philosophizes Upon the War, Etc.," printed after Sherman's March from Atlanta to Savannah that began in November of 1864.

INTERACTIVE ACTIVITY

Use the interactive tools to explore the newspaper columns of Major Charles Henry Smith, penned under the name of Bill Arp.

1. Look at the picture of Charles Henry Smith, who used the pen name Bill Arp, and give students some background about his role in the Confederacy.

2. Click the **Newspaper Excerpts** tab to read the Bill Arp column excerpts.

Activity screens

3. Pause to reflect on the language used and philosophy expressed in the texts. Discuss the connotation of particular phrases and what they suggested at the time, as well as now.

TIPS

- Insert a new page and use the **Pen** tool to write a Letter to the Editor in response.

- Record students reading parts of the columns using the **Microphone** tool, if available.

Grant and Lee at Appomattox: 1865

BACKGROUND INFORMATION

LIEUT. GENERAL U. S. GRANT.

Ulysses S. Grant and Robert E. Lee are the best-known generals of the Civil War. Both made reputations for brilliant soldiering early in the war. Grant became a hero for the Union in February 1862 after capturing Fort Henry and Fort Donelson. Those victories took all of Kentucky and western Tennessee out of Confederate hands. Lee became the Confederacy's leading champion in June 1862 when he drove George B. McClellan's Army of the Potomac back from the gates of Richmond.

Much has been made of the differences between Grant and Lee. Grant was an ordinary man who, though he had attended West Point, failed at almost everything until becoming a general. Lee, on the other hand, was a wealthy Virginia aristocrat who was considered the United States' most promising soldier until he defected to the Confederacy. Some of the differences between the two men are hinted at in the cartes de visite they used. Cartes de visite were calling cards used in the 1860s by the mighty and the humble alike. People collected them in albums and especially treasured cards from famous people that had been autographed.

FEATURED INTERACTIVE ACTIVITY

Use this activity to explore the different roles of Robert E. Lee and Ulysses S. Grant

Purpose: Compare and contrast aspects of Northern and Southern leadership.

1. Look at the *Cartes de Visite* documents together. Discuss what calling cards were and the significance of these two calling cards, using the background information.

2. Click the **Activity** button to begin a sorting activity with the class. Have students drag the descriptions in the right-hand column over to the appropriate column in the T-chart. Correctly placed descriptions will stick; incorrectly placed descriptions will bounce back.

3. Once they've completed the T-chart, encourage students to use the **Pen** tool to add their own facts to each column, drawing on prior knowledge or by doing additional research.

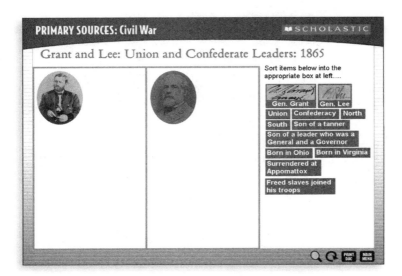

Lee's Surrender: 1865

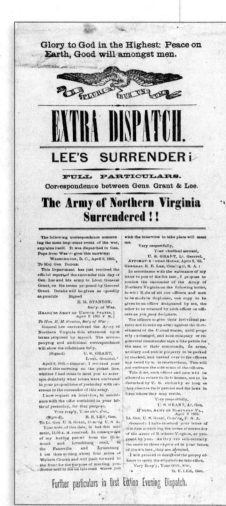

BACKGROUND INFORMATION

By April 1865, Grant and Lee had been fighting head-to-head for nearly a year. Grant suffered enormous casualties, earning him the reputation as a butcher of his own men. But Grant, unlike the eight Union generals who had preceded him, was crushing Lee and the Confederacy. He finally trapped Lee's 35,000-man Army of Northern Virginia near the Appomattox Court House in Virginia. Lee's surrender on April 9, 1865, did not end the war completely; sporadic fighting continued until June. But it did cause the war to end. The jubilation that followed in the North can be seen in the broadside announcing that four brutal years of fighting were over. Newspapers often published broadsides in advance of their regular editions when there was big news.

FEATURED INTERACTIVE ACTIVITY

Use this activity to explore a broadside announcing Lee's surrender, marking the end of the Civil War.

Purpose: Analyze the way news was communicated during this historic moment.

1. Look at the *Extra Dispatch* broadside together. Discuss the context that had led to this moment.

2. Click the **Activity** button and let students fill out the Five W's provided on the chart. Toggle back by clicking on the **Document** button to reread for the answers.

3. After students have written or typed in their responses, click the **Reveal Answer** buttons for one correct way to fill in the chart. Note that students may find other answers in the broadside that are also correct.

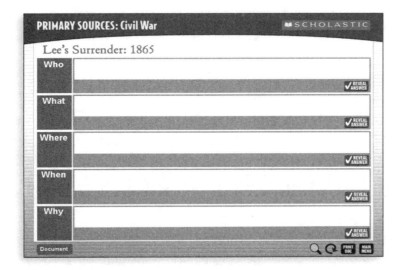

Lincoln's Assassination: 1865

BACKGROUND INFORMATION

The famous actor John Wilkes Booth, a southern sympathizer, shot Abraham Lincoln on April 14, 1865, at Ford's Theater in Washington, D.C. At the time, Lincoln carried two pairs of spectacles (one repaired with a piece of string where the screw had been); a lens polisher; a pocketknife; a watch fob; and a brown leather wallet holding a five-dollar Confederate note as well as nine newspaper clippings. The clippings (not shown in the photograph) included several with positive things to say about Lincoln and his policies. When Lincoln died on the morning of April 15 (at age 56), these personal effects were given to his son Robert Lincoln. The Library of Congress acquired them from a granddaughter of Lincoln in 1937. Included here with these artifacts is an April 15, 1865 front page from *The New York Herald* that carries the report of Lincoln's assassination.

Usually the Library of Congress does not keep personal effects among its holdings, and these items were not put on display until 1976. At the time they were donated, the Librarian of Congress believed that a display of such mundane personal effects might diminish Lincoln's "God-like" status in the eyes of Americans. However, this exhibit continues to be a favorite.

Activity screens

INTERACTIVE ACTIVITY

Use the interactive tools to explore these artifacts of the assassination of President Lincoln.

1. Look at the article published the day after President Lincoln was shot.

2. Click the **Artifacts** tab to see the contents found in President Lincoln's pockets when he was assassinated. Ask students what information the artifacts and headlines provide about Lincoln's death.

TIPS

• Use the **Magnifier** tool to zoom in and read headlines, subheadings, and as much text as possible.

• Reuse the chart from **Lee's Surrender** and fill out the 5 W's for this article.

The Freedman's Second Reader: 1865

BACKGROUND INFORMATION

On March 3, 1865, Congress established a temporary agency called the Bureau of Refugees, Freedmen, and Abandoned Lands, which soon became known as the Freedman's Bureau. It was designed to help the more than four million former slaves adjust to their new lives. O.O. Howard, a Union general famous for his Christian piety, was named its one and only commissioner.

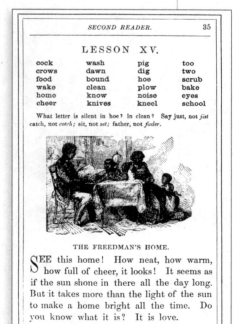

The Bureau wore many hats. It helped set fair wages for black laborers and helped black farmers obtain land. It served as a court system for resolving disputes and often intervened on behalf of former slaves who were threatened with persecution. It registered thousands of black voters and helped an estimated 500,000 people get medical care.

The Bureau's most lasting impact came in the area of education. It helped Northern relief groups like the American Freedman's Union Commission to found schools. By 1869, more than 3,000 schools served more than 150,000 pupils. The Bureau also helped create the first black universities in the South. This exercise shows a page from *The Freedman's Second Reader*, a textbook prepared for freedmen by northern reformers.

In many ways, the Freedman's Bureau was a heartbreaking failure. There was corruption among its 900 or so agents. Also, it's defense of and help for freedmen was often tepid. However, the educational opportunities it provided helped pave the way for future civil rights victories.

INTERACTIVE ACTIVITY

Use the interactive tools to explore this page from a textbook prepared for freedmen by Northern reformers.

1. Look at the exercise from *The Freedman's Second Reader* together.

2. Ask students what they can determine from the content and illustrations about life for the freedmen. What lessons is the text trying to impart to the readers?

TIPS

- Use the **Highlighter** tool to discuss and explore particular phrases and words.

- Use the **Magnifier** tool to zoom in on the illustration. How does it attempt to show a model home?

Activity screens

A Freedman's Second Reader: 1865

A Picture of the Desolated States: 1865–1866

BACKGROUND INFORMATION

In the summer of 1865 and the following winter, northern writer J. T. Trowbridge (1827–1916) made two trips through the defeated South. He visited old battlefields, farms, and burnt-out cities. He spoke to plantation owners, ex-slaves, Union officers, and anyone else who could give him insight into the post-war South.

Trowbridge was an abolitionist who, like many northerners of the time, harbored great anger toward the South over the war. Nevertheless, he wanted to find out how southerners felt and report back to other northerners. The result was a book called *A Picture of the Desolated States.*

At the time of Trowbridge's two visits, feelings from the "late unpleasantness" were still very raw in the South. Union troops occupied all 11 of the rebel states. President Andrew Johnson and Congress were already bickering over how to handle Reconstruction. Nobody was sure how or if the divided country would reunite.

First published in 1866, Trowbridge's book bluntly favored a hard Reconstruction and complete civil rights for former slaves. But he let the voices of southerners—both white and black— come through in his writing. "[This book] is a record of actual observations and conversations," he wrote in the introduction, "free from fictitious coloring."

FEATURED INTERACTIVE ACTIVITY

Use the interactive tools to explore this picture tour of the South after the Civil War.

1. Click the **Picture Tour** button to show a set of photographs with audio narration. **Pause** to discuss the pictures or quotations and descriptions.

2. Click the **Photographs** tab to view each photograph separately.

3. Click the **Web Link** button to read more of J.T. Trowbridge's book, *A Picture of the Desolated States.*

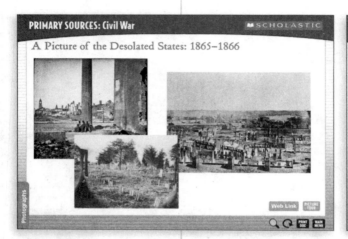

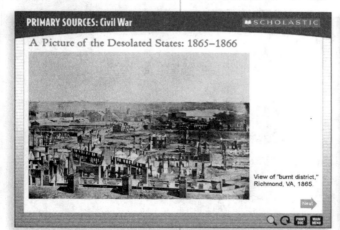

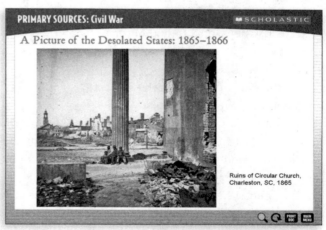

Map of the American Colonies, 1750s

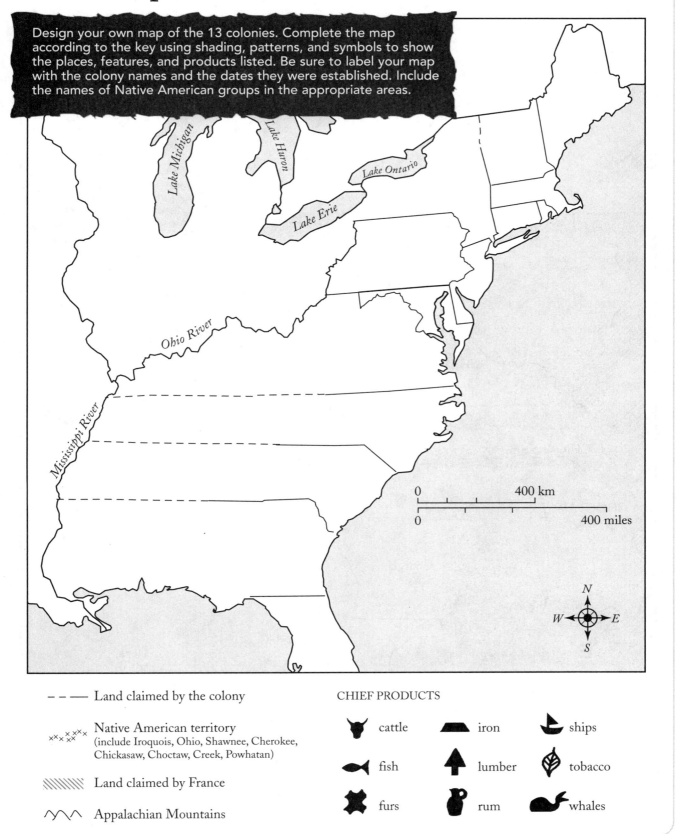

Design your own map of the 13 colonies. Complete the map according to the key using shading, patterns, and symbols to show the places, features, and products listed. Be sure to label your map with the colony names and the dates they were established. Include the names of Native American groups in the appropriate areas.

Lake Michigan

Lake Huron

Lake Ontario

Lake Erie

Ohio River

Mississippi River

0   400 km

0   400 miles

N
W   E
S

– – – Land claimed by the colony

ˣˣˣˣˣ Native American territory
(include Iroquois, Ohio, Shawnee, Cherokee, Chickasaw, Choctaw, Creek, Powhatan)

\\\\\\ Land claimed by France

ⱯⱯⱯ Appalachian Mountains

CHIEF PRODUCTS

cattle   iron   ships

fish   lumber   tobacco

furs   rum   whales

Map of the American Colonies Answer Key

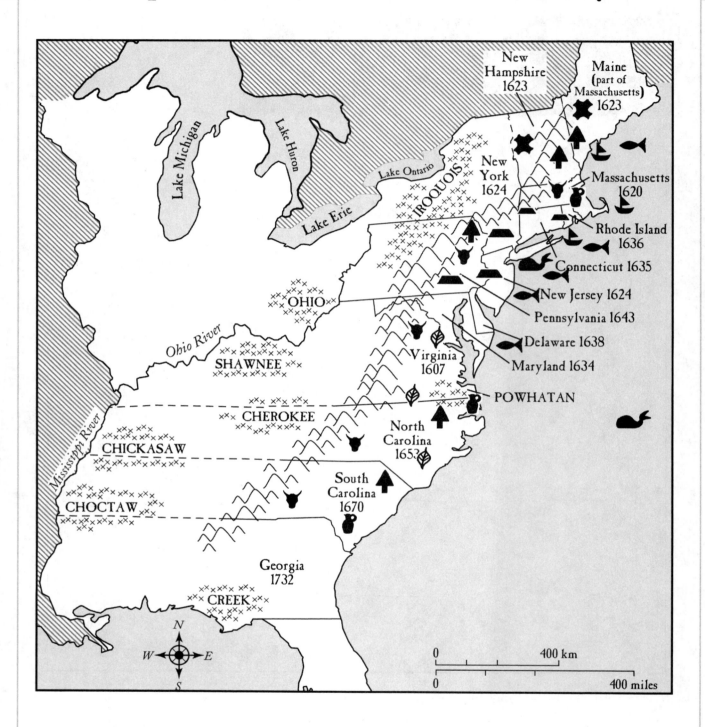

Lake Michigan

Lake Huron

Lake Ontario

Lake Erie

New Hampshire 1623

Maine (part of Massachusetts) 1623

IROQUOIS

New York 1624

Massachusetts 1620

Rhode Island 1636

Connecticut 1635

New Jersey 1624

OHIO

Pennsylvania 1643

Delaware 1638

Maryland 1634

Ohio River

SHAWNEE

Virginia 1607

POWHATAN

North Carolina 1653

CHEROKEE

CHICKASAW

South Carolina 1670

Mississippi River

CHOCTAW

Georgia 1732

CREEK

N
W ● E
S

0   400 km
0   400 miles

Map of the Civil War

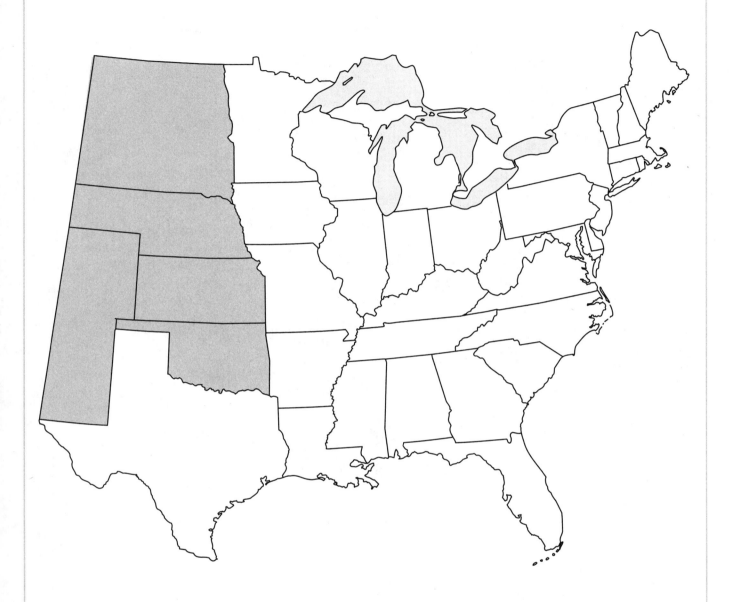

Show what you know about the Union and Confederate states and territories in 1861.

1. Label the states shown on this map. (The shaded states represent territories.)

2. Find the Mason-Dixon Line.

3. Mark the locations of major battles with stars and dates: Bull Run, Gettysburg, Vicksburg, Atlanta, Chattanooga, Antietam, Chancellorsville, Fort Sumter, Mobile Bay, and Appomattox.

4. Color the Union states blue and the Confederate states gray.

Map of the Civil War Answer Key

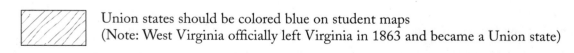
Union states should be colored blue on student maps
(Note: West Virginia officially left Virginia in 1863 and became a Union state)

Confederate states should be colored gray on student maps

Map of the Westward Movement (1800s)

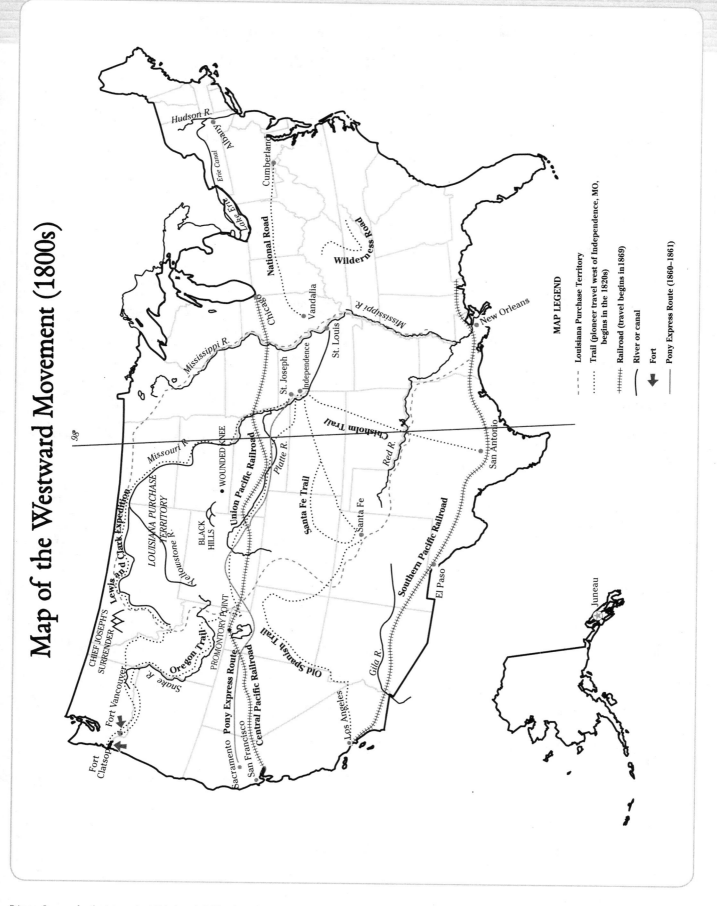

MAP LEGEND

- – – – Louisiana Purchase Territory
- · · · · Trail (pioneer travel west of Independence, MO, begins in the 1820s)
- ┼┼┼┼ Railroad (travel begins in 1869)
- ▼ River or canal
- ▼ Fort
- ——— Pony Express Route (1860–1861)

Hudson R.

Erie Canal

Lake Erie

Cumberland

National Road

Wildern ess **Road**

Chicago

Vandalia

Mississippi R.

St. Louis

New Orleans

Mississippi R.

St. Joseph

Independence

Chisholm Trail

Red R.

San Antonio

Missouri R.

• WOUNDED KNEE

Platte R.

Union Pacific Railroad

Santa Fe Trail

Santa Fe

LOUISIANA PURCHASE TERRITORY

Yellowstone R.

BLACK HILLS

CHIEF JOSEPH'S SURRENDER

Lewis and Clark Expedition

Snake R.

Fort Vancouver

Oregon Trail

PROMONTORY POINT

Pony Express Route

Sacramento

San Francisco

Central Pacific Railroad

Old Spanish Trail

Los Angeles

Gila R.

El Paso

Southern Pacific Railroad

Fort Clatsop

Juneau

98°

Evaluate That Document!

Title or name of document _____

Date of document _____

TYPE OF DOCUMENT:

❏ letter	❏ patent
❏ diary/journal	❏ poster
❏ newspaper article	❏ advertisement
❏ photograph	❏ drawing/painting
❏ map	❏ cartoon
❏ telegram	❏ other _____

POINT OF VIEW:

Who created this document? _____

For whom was this document created? _____

_____

What was the purpose for creating this document? _____

_____

What might the person who created it have been trying to express? _____

_____

What are two things you can learn about the time period from this primary source?

_____

_____

What other questions do you have about this source?

_____

_____

_____

_____